THE ULTIMATE
TEDDY BEAR
BOOK

THE ULTIMATE
TEDDY BEAR
BOOK

PAULINE COCKRILL

Photography by
ROLAND KEMP

Reader's Digest

The Reader's Digest Association (Canada) Ltd.
Montreal

A DORLING KINDERSLEY BOOK

Important Notice
Quotation marks indicate that a
bear's name was given by an owner

Art Editor
Vicki James
Designer
Joanna Pocock
Editors
Susie Behar
Lynne Williams
Senior Art Editor
Gill Della Casa
Senior Editor
Mary-Clare Jerram
Production Controller
Rosalind Priestley

Published in Canada in 1991 by
The Reader's Digest Association (Canada) Ltd.
215 Redfern Avenue, Montreal, Quebec H3Z 2V9

First published in Great Britain in 1991
by Dorling Kindersley Limited,
9 Henrietta Street, London WC2E 8PS

Canadian Cataloguing in Publication Data
Main entry under title:

The Ultimate teddy bear book

Includes index.
ISBN 0-88850-176-5

1. Teddy bears. I. Reader's Digest Association
(Canada)

GV122U.7.O48 1991 688.7'24 C91-090240-2

Computer Page Make-up by The Cooling Brown Partnership, Great Britain
Text Film Output by Creative Input, Great Britain
Reproduced by Colourscan, Singapore
Printed and Bound by Arnoldo Mondadori Editore, Italy

92 93 94 95 / 5 4 3 2

CONTENTS

❧ INTRODUCTION ❧

By Paul and Rosemary Volpp

We refer to today's teds as one of the few "cradle to grave" toys. People purchase teddy bears as crib toys for babies. Young men buy them for their sweethearts as a token of affection. They are used for solace in police cars and hospitals. Dealers buy for profit. And collectors buy them for pure joy!

WHY DO WE COLLECT BEARS?

People collect for such a variety of reasons. We have friends who collect just advertising bears; others collect only those made the year they were born, or only Steiff or Hermann. Paul, my husband, says I collect bears beginning with "a" – a big one, a little one, and so it goes. Actually, we collect variety. Some collectors go for "mint condition." We respond to the way the bear looks at you. Bears should make you feel good. If a bear makes me smile, that is grand. If he or she makes me laugh out loud, he or she will come home with me.

EARLY ACQUISITION

An indescribable thrill comes from purchasing a bear from its original owner. "Mrs. Robinson" (*see p.20*) was our first such bear. We were at a convention in California, in 1982. About noon, I was on my way to buy sandwiches and soft drinks. An elderly, well-dressed lady came up to me. She said she had her childhood bear with her and would I be interested? Interested? I almost fainted! She said she had been standing there for some time, waiting for someone who looked as if they would be kind to her bear. We called the bear "Mrs. Robinson" – after her owner. The real Mrs. Robinson had been given the bear in 1904, when she was very young. Her family was not interested in the bear. So sad! But what good luck for us! I believe that sometimes you don't find bears – they find you!

AUSTRALIAN FIND

Another acquisition story dear to our hearts happened on our second trip to Australia. We went to the Brooks Doll and Teddy Convention in Sydney. We made a guest appearance on the *Today Show* and, as we were leaving, one of the secretaries handed us a note asking us to call a viewer. Paul's call brought us an invitation to visit a lady in a town called Parametta. She was a retired doll and

△ **First Friend**
A photograph dating from 1905 illustrates the role of the teddy bear as a child's earliest and dearest companion and confidante.

△ **Record Breaker**
Bunny Campione of Sotheby's London, holding the Steiff bear "Happy" (see p.45). Paul Volpp, bought the bear as a wedding anniversary present for his wife.

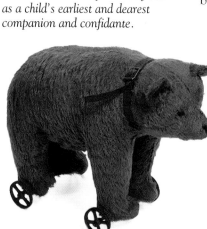

△ **On All Fours**
The teddy bear's ancestor, known as Bruin, is highly collectible. This one was made by Steiff.

▷ **Overbearing Bear**
The teddy bear's "larger than life" personality is captured in this old photograph.

△ **Early Postcard**
Postcards featuring teddy bears, dating from early this century, are in great demand among collectors.

bear collector, and she had some bears that she wanted us to have. As she put it, "the local dealers were waiting for her to die to get her collection." It seemed to delight her tremendously to outsmart them. After a very proper British tea, our host offered to sell us an early J.K. Farnell bear. She had another smaller, later Farnell and, marvel of marvels, a wonderful brown, early Steiff with the "button in ear" still intact (Steiffs in Australia are as rare as hens' teeth). Only one bear, "Paul," had a name. So we decided to call the trio "Peter," "Paul," and "Parametta Mary."

COLLECTING TIPS

How do you start bear collecting? Paul's cardinal rule is to read everything that is available. Read, but also remember! With so much to be taken in, I would recommend *The Ultimate Teddy Bear Book* as a constant shopping companion. Go to "bear stores." As you browse, you can educate yourself. More often than not, you'll leave with a new friend – or at least have one put on "layaway." Attend conventions. Collectors, artists, and dealers from great distances gather together at these great functions. Even if you don't spend a penny, you will increase your knowledge. You can also join teddy bear clubs. We belong to several close to home, where we can attend and learn from the programs, as well as enjoying the fellowship. If you are serious, seek out dealers and tell them what you are looking for. They will get in touch with you if they have any information on the whereabouts of your "want" item. You can also contact auction houses and, for a fee, they will send you their presale catalogs. Looking through these is another good way to get a feel for bear prices. They make great wish books!

▽ **Rare Bear**
Peter, made in 1925 by Gebrüder Süssenguth (see p.44), is rare and valuable.

△ **British Bear**
Early British bears, like this one from the 1930s, are now prized.

◁ **Teddy Ambassadors**
Paul and Rosemary Volpp, with "Dearheart," "Bo" and "Happy." With these Steiff bears, the Volpps have traveled to Australia and England, as well as all corners of the United States.

△ **Pocket-size**
These three 1920s Schuco bears are pocket-size.

TEDDY PARADE

Before World War I, teddy bears were bearlike, with pointed muzzles, humped backs, and long limbs. They were made of mohair plush in realistic colors, with felt pads on their feet and paws, and shoe button eyes. At first, the principal manufacturer was the German company Steiff, although other countries soon jumped on the teddy bear bandwagon with stuffed toy makers of their own. American bears, for example, were different from their British cousins; the English bears had flatter faces, shorter, straighter limbs, and eventually, no humpback. By the late 1940s, many bears were made of synthetic fibers, in less realistic colors, and they were filled with kapok instead of the traditional excelsior stuffing. The shape of the teddy bear changed dramatically – a fatter, unjointed bear was emerging.

NEW BEARS, NEW MATERIALS

In 1954, the first fully machine-washable bear was manufactured, and by the 1960s, most bears were made entirely of synthetic materials. However, the 1980s saw a revival of the traditional teddy bear for the new market of teddy bear collectors. A cottage industry developed, making collectors' bears with natural materials, but in compliance with modern safety standards.

▽ *c. 1918, British*
A British version of Steiff. The bear has shorter limbs, a long thin body, and a pointed muzzle projecting from his forehead.

▷ *c. 1905, German*
This Steiff bear, with his realistic bearlike shape and color, is typical of his time.

▷ *c. 1955, British*
A typical postwar bear with a large head, wide forehead, plastic eyes, stumpy limbs, pads made from Rexine, and excelsior stuffing.

▷ *c. 1963, British*
A machine-washable bear, made by Wendy Boston.

▽ *1950s, British*
A mohair plush bear with velveteen paws, plastic eyes, and bells in his ears.

▽ *1960s, Australian*
This tiny, unjointed teddy was manufactured by the firm Jakas.

▽ **1921, German**
A later Steiff with slightly
shorter, plumper limbs
and glass eyes instead
of the early bears'
shoe buttons.

▽ **1930s, British**
These three bears are typical British
examples of their time. They have
short limbs, flat faces, and velveteen
and woven cotton fabric instead of
felt for foot and paw pads.

▽ **1940s, British**
A Chiltern musical bear made from
artificial silk/rayon plush. After
1930 this material was available in
a variety of colors.

▽ **1940s, British**
Like many wartime bears, this
one is made of sheepskin with
leather pads.

▽ **1970s, American**
An unjointed bear manufactured
with man-made materials by the
Knickerbocker Toy Co.
The parts were sewn
together in Korea.

▽ **1988, American**
The American company Applause
made this modern teddy out of
synthetic plush stuffed with
polyester wadding.

▽ **1987-8, German**
Teddy Rose is one of a limited edition
of 10,000. He is a replica of a Steiff
bear that was originally made in 1925.

▽ **1986, British**
A bear made by the family
firm Canterbury Bears.

▽ **1987, British**
Brian's Bear was made for the
teddy bear shop Asquith's. He
is a fine example of a
collectors' bear.

BEAR FEATURES

The design of the detailed features on a teddy bear – his eyes, his nose, his mouth, and his claws – has changed over the years. In conjunction with the overall shape and the materials used in the construction of his body, the eyes, nose, mouth, and claws can help you determine the date and provenance of a teddy bear, especially if, as is so often the case, no trademark exists.

EYES

Small wooden shoe button

Large wooden shoe button

Shoe button on red felt

Small metal button

Clear glass, painted back

Eyes were held on wire shanks or hooks

NOSE

Hand-stitched in black

Molded gutta-percha

Noses were usually hand-stitched with black or brown thread. An early natural plastic called gutta-percha was used on some bears, notably the rare metal-rodded 1904/5 Steiff.

MOUTH

Stitched, wide smile

The mouths of most bears during this period were the traditional inverted V shape: a single stitch on either side of a central vertical stitch. A few bears like the Columbia Laughing Bear, however, had open mouths revealing a row of teeth.

CLAWS

Four stitches to pad edge

Claws were usually indicated with black or brown thread: four stitches stretched from the edge of the pad across the plush.

Old and New Bears
A Steiff bear dating from the early 1900s (left) sits next to a Steiff bear dating from the 1980s (right).

EYES
Eyes are probably the best indicators of age, although you should be wary of replacements. It can be difficult distinguishing glass from plastic: if you place your lip on an eye, glass will feel colder and harder than plastic.

NOSE
Throughout history, teddy noses have been stitched with thread. The more unusual celluloid, tin, and leather noses often date from before World War II; molded rubber or plastic noses appear on post-1950s bears.

MOUTH
The mouths on the vast majority of bears are suggested with black or brown stitching that forms an inverted V shape. Variations on this theme give the different bears their individual expressions.

CLAWS
Stitching – in a variety of styles – is the most common way of indicating claws on a teddy's feet and paws. Some of the more unusual bears have claws molded on their rubber or wooden pads.

1914–1944　　　　1945–1969　　　　1970–1990

Bulbous,
opaque glass　　*Rolling glass*
set in socket　　*Enameled*
metal button

Bulbous, brown
glass　　*Glass inside*
rubber socket　　*Safe, plastic*
screw-in

Amber plastic　　*Replica shoe*
button　　*Replica metal*
button

Clear glass,
painted back　　*Amber and*
black glass　　*Blue and*
black glass

From around 1955, the plastic screw-in eye was used by most bear manufacturers. The screw-in eye was considered much safer for children than the eyes on wire shanks or hooks that were used previously.

Manufacturers are now required by law to use safe plastic lock-in eyes for children's toys. Glass eyes and plastic replicas of traditional shoe buttons are used for bears aimed at the collectors' market.

Vertical stitching
(Steiff)　　*Painted*
composition　　*Curled leather*

Painted tin　　*Pink stitch*
across　　*Wide,*
rectangular,
stitched

Realistic, molded
plastic　　*Stylized,*
bulbous
plastic

Hand-stitched noses are still the most popular. The style of the stitching varies according to the manufacturer.

Vertical stitching
(Merrythought)　　*Vertical*
stitching

Molded and plastic noses were used during this period.

Narrow, stitched　　*Molded rubber*

Safe plastic lock-in noses are common on children's teddies; bears made for the collectors' market, however, usually have hand-stitched noses.

Stitched, wide,
smiling　　*One stitch*　　*Double stitch*

Traditional
inverted V　　*Open, felt lining*　　*Hinged jaw,*
felt lining

Open, painted
felt tongue　　*Single stitch*

Open, felt
lining　　*Open, teeth,*
moving tongue　　*Open, felt*
lining, tongue

Manufacturers experimented with open and moving mouths, but hand-stitching continued to be the most popular means of indicating a bear's mouth.

Stitched, wide,
smiling

Some open mouths are now operated by microchips installed inside the teddy bears. Collectors' bears usually have stitched mouths.

Stitches across
pad　　*Stitch across*
plush and pad　　*Stitch across*
plush and pad

Molded rubber
with toes　　*Stitches across*
plush and pads　　*Shaggy plush*
conceals claws

Carved,
wooden　　*Stitches*
across pads　　*Stitches*
across plush

Blanket stitch

J.K. Farnell, W.J. Terry, and Merrythought gave their bears joined claws (blanket stitching). Unjoined claws remained the most popular, sometimes reaching across the pad and the plush.

Stitches in the traditional style across the plush, the pads, or plush and pads, are still used for indicating claws. There are variations, however. Bears designed by Robert Raikes have claws carved into their wooden foot and paw pads.

THE TEDDY IS BORN

We can thank the 26th President of the United States, Theodore, or Teddy, Roosevelt, for giving the teddy bear his name. In November 1902, this popular family man took a four-day break from politics to attend a bear hunt in Mississippi. The President was unlucky, and his only chance of a kill was a bear cub cornered and tied to a tree. He refused to shoot it. The incident was illustrated in the Washington Post by the political cartoonist Clifford K. Berryman. Through Berryman, the little bear came to symbolize the President and was featured in many of the artist's subsequent cartoons. Within a year, the cartoon bear had been transformed into a toy for children – the teddy bear.

A PRESIDENT'S MASCOT

Before the introduction of the teddy bear, the burgeoning toy industry of the 1880s had used the bear as a subject for automatons. These clockwork bears, which could dance, drink, or smoke, were very popular. Many originated from French manufacturers, such as Descamps and Martin. In Germany, more realistic stuffed toy bears that stood on all fours and sometimes moved on wheels were made. There is no doubt, however, that it was as a mascot for President Roosevelt that the teddy bear *per se* came into being. A year after Berryman's cartoon, two Russian émigrés, Morris and Rose Michtom, transformed the cartoon bear into a jointed, plush teddy bear. The Michtoms sold their stock of bears to the wholesalers Butler Bros. and founded The Ideal Novelty and Toy Co., the highly successful toy manufacturer.

△ **Drinking Bear**
An early clockwork drinking bear.

△ **Cartoon**
Berryman's original cartoon, depicting Teddy Roosevelt.

STEIFF ORIGINS

At the same time, jointed plush bears were being developed in Germany by a family business headed by Margarete Steiff. Confined to a wheelchair after a childhood bout of polio, she had become an expert seamstress, making children's clothes. In 1880 she formed a mail order company making stuffed toys and other items. The first was a pincushion elephant, an animal that was to appear on Steiff's original trademark. At first, the Steiff bears were unsuccessful, until the Leipzig Fair in March 1903, when Hermann Berg, a toy buyer for the New York department store George Borgfeldt and Co., bought 3,000 teddy bears. In 1905, the Steiff bear was legally protected by the famous "button in ear" trademark. He was so popular that the factory was forced to expand three times between 1903 and 1908. During this period, known as the *Barenjahre* (Bear Years), the number of teddy bears produced annually rose dramatically, from 12,000 to about 975,000 – a phenomenal figure

△ **Founder**
Margarete Steiff.

△ **Theodore Roosevelt**
The original Teddy, greatly loved by the American people.

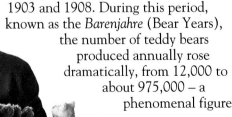

◁ **Steiff Factory**
In 1950, the Steiff factory at Giengen am Brenz employed about 2,000 workers to make teddy bears.

△ **Teddy B and Teddy G**
Seymour Eaton's bears appeared in 20 American newspapers.

△ **Model Bears**
Teddy bears soon became important photographic accessories.

never since repeated. The teddy bear's popularity was boosted by the introduction of Seymour Eaton's *Roosevelt Bears*. These rhyming tales originally appeared in Sunday newspapers starting in 1905, and were then published in four books between 1906 and 1907. The tales started with *The Roosevelt Bears, their Travels and Adventures*, which inspired many novelties such as mugs, spoons, and books. By about 1907, Teddy's Bear was universally known as the teddy bear and had become well established in the home.

GERMANY AND THE UNITED STATES
Stuffed toy manufacturers in both Europe and the United States increased in numbers in an attempt to keep up with growing demand. In Germany, the center of the toy industry, many doll and toy firms, such as Gebrüder Bing, Fleischmann, and Bloedel turned their attention to making teddy bears. In 1907, stimulated by the teddy bear phenomenon, Johann Hermann founded his world famous stuffed toy factory. In the United States, the demand for teddy bears was met similarly. Toy firms like the American Doll and Toy Manufacturing Co. began producing mohair plush bears in about 1906. Other manufacturers, such as Hahn & Amberg, originally a maker of leather goods, also turned to teddy bears. Some companies, such as Aetna and Bruin, were short-lived, but all tried to equal the imported Steiff bears, as revealed in advertisements by Hecla and the Miller Manufacturing Co.

BRITISH TEDDIES
In Britain, the teddy bear enjoyed considerable success. He first appeared in 1909 in a children's story, *The Tale of Teddy Bright Eyes*. It is possible that the toy's success was also fueled by the country's own "Teddy," King Edward VII. The majority of teddy bears originated at the Steiff factory in Germany, but a handful of stuffed toy manufacturers established in the late nineteenth century, principally the London-based companies, William J. Terry (est.1890), the British United Toy Manufacturing Co. (est.1894), and J.K. Farnell (est.1897), made some bears. In 1903, Henry Samuel Dean established Dean's Rag Book Co. near London's Fleet Street. Along with the cloth books "for children who wear their food and eat their clothes," it produced various printed cotton toys, including teddy bears. Its first plush bears were not introduced until just before World War I.

△ **Cutouts**
Printed cotton cutout bear, patented in 1905 by the British Dean's Rag Book Co.

△ **Trademarks**
The trademarks of the British United Manufacturing Co., and Aetna Toy Animal Co.

▽ **Terryer Toys**
A dog was the trademark of British stuffed toy manufacturer William J. Terry.

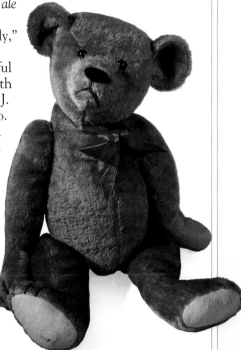

△ **Heirloom**
Probably one of the original Ideal bears, this bear was presented to Roosevelt's grandson. It now lives in Washington D.C., in the Smithsonian Institution.

Bear Necessities

W ith few exceptions, early teddy bears were made from natural materials: mohair plush fabric, excelsior stuffing, shoe button eyes, felt paws, and embroidered details. After experimentation, a joint system, giving bears a mobile head and limbs, was perfected, and a squeaker or growler mechanism became an essential requirement.

EYES
Wooden shoe button eyes with metal loops on the back were sewn into the bear's face. Some British firms preferred black metal buttons. Miniature bears were given small glass bead eyes on wire shanks.

Wooden shoe buttons

White mohair plush

Golden mohair plush

Glass bead eye

Glass eye on wire shank

Pairs of glass eyes joined by lengths of wire

FUR FABRICS
Toy animals had been made from real fur, but with the introduction of the teddy bear, mohair plush, a cheaper imitation fabric, was invented. Soft, silky, and dirt-resistant, it is woven from the fleece of the angora goat.

1905 STEIFF
This bear is typical of the period, with his brown mohair plush and shoe button eyes.

Brown mohair plush

BURLAP
A few early bears were made from burlap, a brown, coarsely woven material. Produced from jute, a fiber found in tree bark, it was imported from the Indian subcontinent.

Burlap

Felt scrap

BOARD JOINTS
One cardboard disk was attached to the limb, the other was part of the main body. Both disks rotated on a small pin, inserted through a metal washer. A felt scrap acted as a buffer between the disks.

Cardboard disks

Small pin *Metal washer*

Cotter pin

METAL JOINTS
Sometimes metal disks were used with cardboard disks to give the jointing system greater strength. The disks rotated on a cotter pin (with double prongs that splayed out).

Cotton thread

SEAM THREAD
After the bear had been stuffed, very strong thread was used for hand-sewing the final openings of the body, head, and tops of limbs.

Metal and cardboard disks

MOLDED NOSE
Some early bears had molded noses that were made from gutta-percha – a natural plastic.

Gutta-percha

Embroidery silks

Cotton thread

Felt

HAND-STITCHED DETAILS
Thick embroidery silk created countless noses, mouths, and claws. The individual parts of the bear were machine-stitched with cotton thread to match the mohair plush.

FELT PADS
Paw and foot pads on early bears were made of felt. The most common colors were beige and cream, although black was sometimes used for black bears. (Colored felt was often used to reinforce the pads.)

TILT GROWLER
In 1908 tilt growlers were introduced. Contained in a cardboard tube, a lead weight opened or closed the bellows when the bear was tilted, forcing air over the reed and so creating a growl.

Lead weight

PUNCH GROWLER
One of the earliest voice boxes consisted of a bag of oilcloth. When the bear's stomach, containing the bag, was punched, a rush of air caused the reed inside to vibrate.

Bellows made with wood and oilcloth

Oilcloth bag

EXCELSIOR STUFFING
Also known as straw stuffing, excelsior is made from long, fine-quality wood shavings, previously used as a packing material for delicate objects such as china. Cork granules, another packing material, provided an alternative stuffing for printed cloth bears.

Excelsior

Gauze speaker

Cardboard container holding tilt growler

REED
The same type of reed was used in growlers and squeakers.

Reed contained within tubing

Oilcloth strip binding

KAPOK PACKING
Kapok is a protective, silky fiber that comes from the seed pod of a tropical tree. Steiff used it as a packing around voice boxes.

Kapok

Coiled spring

SQUEAKER
Squeakers were used before tilt growlers. When the bear's stomach was squeezed, air vibrated the reed that was attached to the underside of one of the pieces of wood or cardboard.

BEAR APPAREL

*T*he clothes a child chooses for his or her teddy bear can provide an insight into the relationship between the two of them. A child's instinct to treat a bear like a human, and dress it, presented manufacturers with an opportunity they could not afford to miss. The teddy's doll-like, jointed body made him ideal for outfits of every conceivable form, and as soon as 1906 teddy bear manufacturers had set about clothing him. Steiff produced a series of dressed bears that included Basa and Basi in sailor suits or dresses, and Batro, who wore a knitted suit and cap.

BEARS FOR THE BOYS

In the United States, the teddy bear was marketed as the boy's toy, as an alternative to his sister's doll, and so commercially made clothes often reflected his masculine character: there were suits for policemen, firemen, and sailor bears, and Rough Rider outfits – the uniform of Roosevelt's U.S. volunteer cavalry – were also popular. Steiff, D.W. Shoyer and Co., and Kahn and Mossbacher all produced suits with the names of Teddy B and Teddy G (*see pp.12-13*) embroidered on the chest or sleeve.

△ **Top Hat**
An Edwardian salesman's sample, found in an antique market, makes an obvious accessory for an aristocratic bear.

△ **The Casual Look**
A 1906 Steiff bear wearing a double-breasted knitted suit with brass buttons.

IMPROVISED OUTFITS

Garments designed especially for teddy bears were expensive in the early 1900s. So naturally, children and parents often made the clothes themselves, using patterns found in such magazines as the *Ladies Home Journal*, *The Delineator*, and *The Woman's Home Companion*. Homemade outfits, based on contemporary clothing, were common, and the cast-offs of dolls or babies were also useful. University students dressed their bears in knitted suits consisting of a sweater, trousers, and a cap, all in the appropriate college colors. As few of the teddy clothes made in the early 1900s have survived today, collectors tend to seek out Edwardian baby clothing, such as bonnets and gowns, and period accessories: bags, watches, and jewelry. Dressing teddy bears is very enjoyable, but there are also some less obvious advantages to be gained from this practice: clothes protect a bear from dust and light, and also help disguise the fact that he or she may be missing a limb or two.

△ **Scholarly Bear**
The addition of accessories, preferably contemporary, adds greatly to a bear's personality. This 1905 Steiff with mortarboard and satchel would have appealed enormously to schoolchildren and students.

△ **Edwardian Chic**
An Edwardian child's bonnet and bloomers, made from broderie anglaise and lace-trimmed cotton, evokes a bygone era.

◁ **The Cattley Toys**
Now in London's Bethnal Green Museum of Childhood, this collection dates from about 1906. The teddy bears originally belonged to five children of the Cattley family, who created all their bear outfits themselves. They made full sets of underwear, using remnants of broderie anglaise, velvet, and lace.

▷ **Nautical Teddy**
A 1911 bear proudly shows off a World War I naval uniform and an unusual hand-stitched shirt.

BEAR MEMORABILIA

The craze for the teddy bear, and all things related, is not a recent phenomenon. As early as 1907, the teddy bear's popularity was reaching great heights, and stuffed toy makers competed to produce bears with additional novelty appeal, such as teddies with reversible heads. Other factories specialized in producing metal, china, wood, rubber, and celluloid bears. In the United States, the teddy bear's influence was so pervasive that bears appeared on postcards, advertising material, and song sheets. Over 400 copyrights for song titles using the words "teddy" or "teddy bear" were registered between 1907 and 1911.

△ Teething Ring
The hollow silver teddy bear with ball bearings and a bone teething ring dates from 1910.

NOVELTY BEARS

Almost from the beginning, teddy bears that could squeak or growl were made, but it was not long before manufacturers attempted to produce something a little different. In 1907 the Self-whistling Bear, which whistled when turned upside down, and the Musical Bear, with a turn handle music box, were produced by Strauss, the "toy king" of New York. From New York, too, came the Columbia Teddy Bear Manufacturers' Laughing Bear, with open jaws of pointed teeth, and the Electric Bright Eye Bear, patented on February 19, 1907, by the Fast Black Skirt Co. The Electric Bright Eye Bear had red or white eyes that lit up when its right paw was squeezed. Various moving teddy bears were also made, some with no clockwork mechanism, such as Mrs. Gillespie's Tumbling Bear of New York. In 1911, in Germany, a fierce legal battle ensued between two manufacturers, Steiff and Bing, over the patent on two similar somersaulting clockwork bears.

In 1913, Steiff made a bear, known as the Record Bear, which could be pulled along on a four-wheeled metal chassis, with a squeaker on the rear axle.

△ Bisque Bear
An unglazed porcelain bear with jointed limbs.

△ Teddy Buttons
Mohair plush coats with teddy bear brass buttons were popular with children around 1907.

△ Sheet Music
A detail from the front cover of the sheet music for The Teddy Bears Frolic, *published in London in 1910.*

▽ Bear In A Box
Miniature bears were popular from the outset. This example, with his own trunk, was originally bought in a street market.

FROM RATTLES TO JUMPING JACKS

Teddy bears were featured on nursery items, including babies' ceramic bowls, throughout this period. Silver baby spoons were embossed with teddy bears climbing the handle or engraved on the bowl. Rattles designed as fur fabric sticks with a teddy bear head at each end were made, although particularly collectible (and possibly more useful) are the silver bear-motif rattles and teething rings. One of the "bearskin" (mohair plush) coats for young children, made from black, brown, white, or blue mohair, with teddy bear-embossed brass buttons, is a rare find. Another sought-after item is the Steiff hot water bottle of 1909. This was made in the shape of a traditional jointed bear with a tin canister inside, accessible through a laced-up central front seam. Teddy bear-inspired board, card, and parlor games abounded, as did teddy ABC blocks, chime toys, money boxes, jumping jacks, tea sets, and jewelery.

△ English Plate
This 1912 child's plate shows a popular design.

▽ Clothing
The muff shown below is worn by its original young owner. The photograph dates from between 1905 and 1910.

◁ Acrobatic Bear
Similar to the Steiff tumbling bear (see p.40), this rare Bing clockwork bear dating from about 1910 performs acrobatic feats when his arms are rotated.

△ Teddy Bear Muff
Several manufacturers, including Steiff, made children's muffs in the shape of fat teddy bears.

❧ "Mrs. Robinson" ❧
1904 IDEAL NOVELTY & TOY CO.

"Mrs. Robinson" is said to be one of the early teddy prototypes manufactured by the Ideal Novelty & Toy Co., the first company to produce teddy bears in the United States. In 1938, it became the highly successful Ideal Toy Corporation, which was taken over by CBS in 1982. At that time, sadly, teddy bears were discontinued.

EARS
Ideal bears usually have much rounder ears than those of "Mrs. Robinson."

EYES
Like so many of the teddy bears made before World War I, "Mrs. Robinson" has black wooden shoe button eyes, sewn just inside the seam of her face.

Long protruding muzzle

CLAWS
Each foot and paw has four claws, embroidered in a double thickness of light brown thread.

FEET
Her feet are neither as long nor as narrow as those belonging to her Steiff cousins. The oval pads are covered with beige felt, reinforced with cardboard.

The pads of early Ideal bears were narrow at the toe ends

Bear profile *A large rounded head, gentle sloping forehead, and peculiarly accentuated hump on the back make "Mrs. Robinson" distinct from her American contemporaries.*

NOSE
The triangular nose of rust-colored broadcloth, secured with stitching of the same color, is the work of a repairer. The original would have been hand-stitched in the same brown thread as her mouth and claws.

ARMS
"Mrs. Robinson's" long tapering arms are curved at the paw ends, much like those of the early Steiff bears.

Beige mohair plush

• BEAR ESSENTIALS •

HT: 17in (42cm)

FUR: beige-colored, mohair plush
EYES: small, black, wooden, shoe buttons
EARS: large, placed wide apart and low
MUZZLE: long, protruding, and pointed

NOSE: broadcloth, triangular, rust
ARMS: long, curved; beige felt pads; claws
FEET: large, oval; beige felt pads; claws
STUFFING: excelsior throughout bear

DISTINGUISHING FEATURES: The unique, upwardly pointing hump projecting out from "Mrs. Robinson's" back sets her apart from contemporary American bears.

❧ *"Eddie"* ❧

c. 1903-1905 STEIFF

The blank, nickel-plated button in "Eddie's" left ear represents the prototype of Steiff's now famous trademark. Originally the idea of Richard Steiff's younger brother, Franz, the button was stamped for a brief period with the elephant logo. The word "Steiff" was introduced on May 13, 1905, the year the button was patented.

Slightly curved ears

EARS
"Eddie" has little rounded ears, placed wide apart at a diagonal on his now balding head.

EYES
The small wooden shoe button eyes are close-set, adding considerably to his appeal.

Thin, black thread mouth

VOICE BOX
Although the squeaker no longer works, its oval shape can be felt beneath the fur fabric. Leather squeakers were often used in early Steiff teddy bears; the tilt growler was not employed until 1908.

ARMS
"Eddie's" long, curved arms taper toward the paws. The balding patch on his right arm may mark the spot where he was frequently clutched by an affectionate owner.

Hand-embroidered, black thread claws

CLAWS
On both feet and paws, the four claws reach from the edge of the pads onto the plush.

FEET
"Eddie's" right foot displays a replacement pad; the original pad on the left foot shows signs of age.

Unusually long muzzle

Bear profile *"Eddie's" rounded head, long muzzle, and humped back create the image of a grand old man.*

NOSE
The triangular nose of horizontal stitches in black thread, outlined with two diagonal stitches, is typically Steiff.

TRADEMARK
Blank Steiff buttons can be an unreliable way of dating a bear, as such buttons were used at various stages throughout the company's history.

Original pad made from beige felt

• BEAR ESSENTIALS •

HT: 13in (33cm)

FUR: beige-colored, worn, mohair plush
EYES: small, wooden, shoe buttons, close-set
EARS: small, rounded, set wide apart
MUZZLE: thin and long, protruding

NOSE: hand-embroidered, triangular, black
ARMS: long, curved; beige felt pads; claws
FEET: large, narrow; beige felt pads; claws
STUFFING: excelsior throughout bear

Blank button

Trademark

❧ *"Oscar"* ❧

1904-1905 STEIFF

After the 1903 Leipzig Fair, Richard Steiff created two new bears, both with gutta-percha noses. The Bär 35 PB still had thread joints, but Bär 28 PB, of which "Oscar" is an example, had metal rods – a system of movement patented in 1905. Bär 28 PB was available only for a brief period and is therefore rare.

Horizontal, ear-to-ear seam

EARS
His ears are made from two semicircles of plush material, sewn into seams on both the sides and the top of his head.

EYES
Wooden shoe buttons, painted black, are sewn just on the outer side of each of the bear's two face seams.

VOICE BOX
These early metal-jointed bears were mute, as growlers were not put in Steiff bears until about 1905.

JOINTS
"Oscar" has a pair of metal rods with cardboard disks at the ends running horizontally through his body. These rods join his legs and arms. Another metal rod extends vertically from the middle of the upper rod, connecting his body and head.

Worn pads show excelsior stuffing

FEET
Like many bears of this early period, his feet are large and pointed.

Mouth was probably an inverted V

Bear profile The side view clearly shows his prominent humped back and long, curved arms. Also visible is his closely clipped, almost foxlike muzzle, with its well-defined molded nose.

NOSE
His lifelike nose is made of gutta-percha, an early type of natural plastic that was also used for making household items such as buckets.

CLAWS
Black thread is used to embroider the five claws. After 1905, Steiff bears were given only four claws.

Long, curved paws

STUFFING
"Oscar" is filled with wood shavings throughout. As in all Steiff bears, the final opening is the center seam at the front. This is hand-sewn using strong thread.

• BEAR ESSENTIALS •

HT: 16in (40cm)

FUR: beige, mohair plush, some clipped short
EYES: small, black, wooden shoe buttons
EARS: small, unstuffed, placed wide apart
MUZZLE: long, tapering, plush clipped short

NOSE: gutta-percha, lifelike, oval, black
ARMS: long, tapered; beige felt pads; claws
FEET: long, pointed; beige felt pads; claws
STUFFING: excelsior throughout bear

Elephant button

Trademark

⚘ "Friend Petz" ⚘

1903-1905 STEIFF

Still known as Bärle in the catalogs, and not yet as the teddy bear, by 1905 Steiff's creation had become less like a bear and more like a bear doll. It now had a refined swivel joint system, a voice box, and rounder features. Various sizes and colors were produced, and the famous trademark "button in ear" was patented.

EARS
This bear is particularly unusual because of his ears. They are large and flat, and sit low on the sides of his head.

EYES
As in most of the early bears, shoe buttons are used as eyes.

Clipped mohair plush muzzle

VOICE BOX
Sadly, in the older bears, the voice box tends not to work anymore. Prodding or shaking the poor creatures is the only way of checking if they have one.

Long, tapering arms

FEET
"Friend Petz" has the long, narrow feet – and shapely ankles – typical of this period. The red felt reinforcement, commonly used in early Steiff bears, can be seen poking through the felt pads.

Beige felt pads repaired with stitching

Bear profile *A side view of "Friend Petz" shows the main features of these early, solid, rounded bears: humpback, pointed muzzle, long, curved limbs, and large feet.*

NOSE AND MOUTH
Both of these have been hand-embroidered in a beige thread, using vertical stitches.

Beige, shaggy mohair plush

PAWS
His spoonlike paws curve upward and have beige felt pads.

CLAWS
The claws are outlined in the same beige thread that is used for the mouth and nose.

• BEAR ESSENTIALS •

HT: 25in (65cm)

FUR: beige, somewhat shaggy, mohair plush
EYES: large, black, shoe buttons, close-set
EARS: large, flat, unstuffed, on sides of head
MUZZLE: long, tapering, short clipped plush

NOSE: hand-embroidered, heart-shaped, beige
ARMS: long, curved; beige felt pads; claws
FEET: long, narrow; beige felt pads; claws
STUFFING: excelsior throughout bear

TRADEMARK: Originally this beige, shaggy bear would have had a Steiff button and label in its ear for easy identification, but sadly, they are missing from "Friend Petz."

❦ "Maximilian" ❦

1905 STEIFF

*Named "Maximilian" by an early owner, this Steiff shares many of the characteristics of "Friend Petz"
(see p.23). However, by 1905 the classic Steiff bear shape was becoming less naturalistic, and "Maximilian"
has a smaller hump and more rounded muzzle than his cousin.*

EARS
Compared with those of earlier
bears, his ears have changed
noticeably, both in shape and
in the angle at which they are
positioned on his head.

HEAD
"Maximilian" has a central seam running
down his muzzle, a common feature in
early Steiffs though rare in teddy bears
generally. The seam exists because the size
of the bear's pattern allowed only six
complete heads to be cut out of each
length of mohair. The seventh
head was, therefore, always cut in
halves, resulting in a seam in the
bear's face.

PADS
All of his pads have been
replaced with new dark
brown felt in an attempt
to combat excess wear
and tear.

*Black wooden
shoe button eyes*

*Bear profile His muzzle and hump seem to be
less prominent than those of "Friend Petz,"
resembling the more doll-related toy the teddy
bear would soon become.*

NOSE AND MOUTH
Both were recently replaced
in black wool, although a
similar black thread
would have been
used originally.

*Green necktie adds
a touch of formality*

FUR
The curly
cinnamon
mohair plush
is in mint
condition.

*The original
felt would have
been lighter*

*Thin ankles
and narrow feet*

• BEAR ESSENTIALS •

FUR: cinnamon-colored, curly mohair plush
EYES: rounded, black, wooden shoe buttons
EARS: small, unstuffed, placed high on head
HT: 22in (56cm)   MUZZLE: pronounced but blunt, fur clipped

NOSE: hand-embroidered, rectangular, black
ARMS: long; brown felt pads; no claws
FEET: narrow; brown felt pads; no claws
STUFFING: excelsior throughout bear

Raised lettering

Trademark

❧ "Blissful" ❧

1907 BRUIN MANUFACTURING CO.

Despite importing thousands of teddy bears from Germany, by 1907 the United States had established numerous firms to keep up with the demand for the Roosevelt-inspired mascots. Few early American bears can be positively identified, but "Blissful" carries the label of the short-lived Bruin Manufacturing Co.

EARS
Like Ideal's "Mrs. Robinson" (*see p.20*), his ears are set well apart, above his very wide forehead and part of the way down the sides of his head. However, his ears are smaller.

EYES
Like many teddy bears of this early period, "Blissful" has black wooden shoe button eyes.

VOICE BOX
There is a worn patch on his stomach where his squeaker has been pushed repeatedly.

Golden mohair plush

STUFFING
Originally stuffed with excelsior, it seems that at some time in the bear's life a softer filling, perhaps kapok, was also added.

Woven label stitched across right foot

FEET
"Blissful" has large feet that are very long, with pads of beige-colored felt.

Bear profile "Blissful" has a typical early American bear body. His triangular muzzle extends directly from his forehead, and he has a traditional humpback.

NOSE AND MOUTH
The mouth and rectangular nose are represented by stitches of black thread.

ARMS
Wide shoulders run into long arms, tapering to thin, curved paws with beige felt pads.

CLAWS
This bear has four short claws on each foot and paw pad.

Black thread claws sewn to edges of pads

• BEAR ESSENTIALS •

HT: 13in (33cm)

FUR: golden-colored, long, mohair plush
EYES: small, black shoe buttons in face seams
EARS: small, slightly cupped, wide apart
MUZZLE: triangular, extends from forehead

NOSE: hand-embroidered, rectangular, black
ARMS: long, curved; beige felt pads; claws
FEET: large; beige felt pads; claws
STUFFING: excelsior, kapok restuffing

Trademark

❧ "Still Hope" ❧

1907 AETNA TOY ANIMAL CO.

"Still Hope" was manufactured by one of the many American firms set up during this period. Its products also included jointed rabbits and monkeys. He was named after an ancestor of his present owners, a woman who was scalped by American Indians and left for dead, but then recovered and lived to be 110.

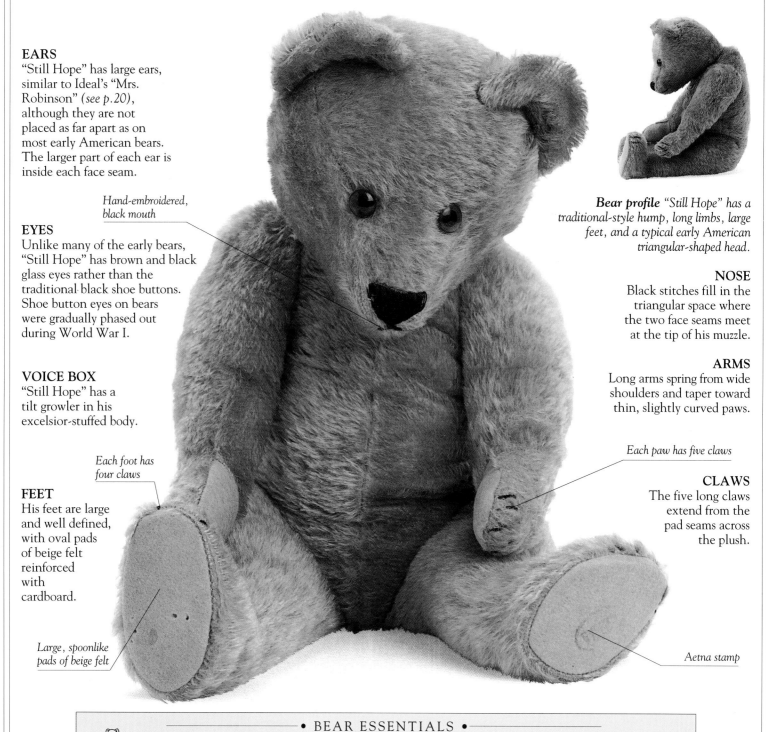

EARS
"Still Hope" has large ears, similar to Ideal's "Mrs. Robinson" (*see p.20*), although they are not placed as far apart as on most early American bears. The larger part of each ear is inside each face seam.

Hand-embroidered, black mouth

EYES
Unlike many of the early bears, "Still Hope" has brown and black glass eyes rather than the traditional black shoe buttons. Shoe button eyes on bears were gradually phased out during World War I.

VOICE BOX
"Still Hope" has a tilt growler in his excelsior-stuffed body.

Each foot has four claws

FEET
His feet are large and well defined, with oval pads of beige felt reinforced with cardboard.

Large, spoonlike pads of beige felt

Bear profile *"Still Hope" has a traditional-style hump, long limbs, large feet, and a typical early American triangular-shaped head.*

NOSE
Black stitches fill in the triangular space where the two face seams meet at the tip of his muzzle.

ARMS
Long arms spring from wide shoulders and taper toward thin, slightly curved paws.

Each paw has five claws

CLAWS
The five long claws extend from the pad seams across the plush.

Aetna stamp

• BEAR ESSENTIALS •

HT: 20in (50cm)

FUR: beige, somewhat worn, mohair plush
EYES: large, brown and black, glass, close-set
EARS: large, set into facial seams across head
MUZZLE: protruding, extension of forehead

NOSE: hand-embroidered, triangular, black
ARMS: long, curved; beige felt pads; claws
FEET: large; beige felt pads; claws
STUFFING: excelsior throughout bear

TRADEMARK: An ink stamp bearing the company's trade name, Aetna, set in an oval black line, is imprinted on the center of the bear's left foot pad.

❧ "Wistful" ❧

1907 BRUIN MANUFACTURING CO.

Although unmarked, "Wistful" is thought to have been made in New York by Bruin, whose rivals in the city included Ideal, Aetna, the Harman Manufacturing Co., and the American Doll and Toy Manufacturing Co. At first, mohair plush was imported from Europe, but soon the United States began to set up its own mills.

EARS
"Wistful" has small rounded ears, although as on Bruin's "Blissful" *(see p.25),* they sit wide apart on his expansive forehead.

Edges of ears just caught into the face seams

EYES
Unlike "Blissful," "Wistful" has brown and black glass eyes, one of which is probably a replacement. They are sewn into the seams running from his ears to his nose.

Mouth curves upward

FUR
His long, golden mohair plush was probably produced locally. In the U.S. at this time, thousands of angora goats were raised just to meet the growing demand for teddy bear fur. His muzzle is covered with the same mohair as his head and body.

Short black claws

FEET
His feet are large and slightly narrower than those of the other early American bears. They have long beige felt pads.

Bear profile "Wistful" has a foxlike face, with a sharp, triangular muzzle. His elongated body is typical of the early American bear.

Replacement glass eye

NOSE
The end of his muzzle is bound with vertical stitches of black thread that form a long, rectangular nose. This is the work of a repairer.

Well-worn muzzle

ARMS
"Wistful" has long and tapering arms that curve at the point where they merge into paws. The paws have large beige felt pads.

CLAWS
Five embroidered black claws are on both the feet and paws. The relatively short stitches extend only from the seam edges across the plush.

Beige felt pads are well worn

• BEAR ESSENTIALS •

HT: 14in (37cm)

FUR: golden-colored, long, mohair plush
EYES: small, brown with black pupils, glass
EARS: small, rounded, set wide apart in seams
MUZZLE: protruding, extension of forehead

NOSE: hand-embroidered, rectangular, black
ARMS: long, tapering; beige felt pads; claws
FEET: large, narrow; beige felt pads; claws
STUFFING: excelsior throughout bear

DISTINGUISHING FEATURES: The unusual long and rectangular nose of this golden bear differs from more common square noses. The vertical stitching is repair work.

❧ "Avalon" ❧

c. 1910 GEBRUDER BING

After 1905, the demand for teddy bears began to soar dramatically, and, in response, the German manufacturer Gebrüder Bing produced its own version of a bear. The company had been making tin housewares since 1865 and had turned to the production of enameled and clockwork toys at the end of the nineteenth century.

EARS
Unlike most Steiff bears of the time, "Avalon's" ears sit quite far down his forehead.

Distinctly curved head

Round, rigid ears

EYES
The replacements are in keeping with the original black shoe buttons.

NOSE AND MOUTH
The black vertical stitches representing the nose are original, but the mouth has been repaired using matching black thread.

Bear profile In shape, this Bing bear is noticeably rounder than his contemporaries. His legs and feet are stumpier than those on Steiff bears.

FUR
The curly mohair plush is in superb condition, although his clipped muzzle is a little worn in places.

Elegant felt-covered paws

CLAWS
"Avalon" still has four black thread claws on each foot. The claws on his paws, however, have become unstitched.

ARMS
The slightly curved arms are in the tradition of early bears.

FEET
Beige felt pads are reinforced with thick cardboard so that "Avalon" can stand upright.

• BEAR ESSENTIALS •

HT: 23in (57cm)

FUR: beige-colored, curly, mohair plush
EYES: medium, black, plastic, shoe buttons
EARS: small, round, high over face seams
MUZZLE: blunt, protruding, clipped mohair

NOSE: hand-embroidered, black thread
ARMS: long; beige felt pads; claws
FEET: large, oval; beige felt pads; claws
STUFFING: excelsior throughout bear

TRADEMARK: Originally bears like "Avalon" would have had a metal arrow tag with GBN on the ear or a button on the body. "Avalon" has the metal arrow tag.

"Bing Oh!"

c. 1911 GEBRUDER BING

In about 1909, Steiff took action to prevent Gebrüder Bing, then probably the largest toy manufacturer in the world, from using a button-in-ear trademark. A metal arrow temporarily replaced the Bing button, until Steiff granted the right for an underarm stud to be used, providing no reference was made to the word "button."

EARS
"Bing Oh!" has large rounded ears. Set wide apart, they sit toward the back and down the sides of his head.

EYES
Traditional black shoe buttons are used for eyes. They are sewn into the facial seams.

Clipped plush muzzle

VOICE BOX
"Bing Oh!" has a tilt growler inside his excelsior-stuffed body.

TRADEMARK
A metal button under this bear's right arm was all that Steiff would allow its rival company to use. The word "button" remained the property of Steiff.

FEET
The very large feet have narrow, extremely long pads similar to those belonging to "Friend Petz" *(see p.23)* and "Maximilian" *(see p.24)*, both early Steiff bears.

Bear profile *From this angle you can see the similarity between "Bing Oh!" and Steiff bears of the same period: the protruding muzzle, humped back, long limbs, and large feet.*

NOSE AND MOUTH
The nose is hand-embroidered with vertical stitches of black thread. His mouth is the traditional inverted V shape with a few vertical stitches joining it to the nose.

ARMS
The long, tapering arms are curved at the paws – similar to those of Steiff bears.

Leather pads replace the original felt pads

Long, dark brown mohair plush

• BEAR ESSENTIALS •

HT: 21in (53cm)

FUR: dark brown, long, mohair plush
EYES: medium, black, wooden, shoe buttons
EARS: large, rounded, placed wide apart
MUZZLE: protruding, clipped mohair plush

NOSE: hand-embroidered, triangular, black
ARMS: curved; brown leather pads; no claws
FEET: large; brown leather pads; no claws
STUFFING: excelsior throughout bear

Trademark

❧ "Miss Nightingale" ❧

1912 BRITISH

Although unmarked, this bear is known to have been made in Britain before World War I. A number of British firms manufactured stuffed toys beginning in the late nineteenth century, using plush produced in the towns of Huddersfield and Dewsbury.

Small rounded ears

EARS
Notice how different these are from those of her German counterparts. The ears are gathered at the bottom, and the whole ear is fitted into the seams of the bear's face.

Metal eyes, instead of the common shoe button eyes

Wide, smiling mouth

EYES
The unusual eyes consist of two round, convex pieces of metal, painted black. Hooks on the backs of the eyes are sewn into the seam at the point where her face merges with her muzzle.

NOSE AND MOUTH
A few horizontal stitches of thin black woolen thread make up her nose and mouth.

Short-pile, golden mohair plush

FEET
These are considerably smaller and rounder than those of Steiff bears from this period. The beige felt pads are pear-shaped and are not lined. The left one looks worn; the right one has been replaced.

Bear profile "Miss Nightingale" looks long and thin in profile. There is only a slight suggestion of a hump on her back – a complete contrast to other bears of the period.

HEAD
The triangular shape of the head and the wide, high forehead make her more like her American than her German cousins.

CLAWS
Each foot and paw displays the remains of five black-thread stitched claws.

Arms are shorter and straighter than those on her German contemporaries

LEGS
The legs appear to have been made from straight pieces of cloth.

• BEAR ESSENTIALS •

HT: 19in (47cm)

FUR: golden, short-pile, mohair plush
EYES: small, black, metal buttons
EARS: small, rounded, gathered at base
MUZZLE: pointed, thin, down-turned

NOSE: hand-embroidered, rectangular, black
ARMS: tapering; beige felt pads; claws
FEET: short; beige felt pads; claws
STUFFING: excelsior throughout bear

DISTINGUISHING FEATURES: This straight, thin bear has a long, narrow-hipped, wide-chested body, and relatively short arms, compared with her contemporaries.

❧ *"Marmaduke"* ❧

c. 1913 WILLIAM J. TERRY

This bear is said to have been made by William J. Terry, one of the early innovators in the British stuffed toy industry. A photograph exists of similar teddies made by this London-based firm, showing them for sale in the city's first department store, Whiteleys.

EARS
His semicircular ears are wider than the small, pert ones of the 1912 British bear (*see p.30*), but are similarly perched in each corner of his triangular-shaped head.

Large eyes give an appealing wide-eyed expression

EYES
The backs of his clear glass eyes are painted an unusual shade of pink. Toy catalog photographs of this time show glass eyes in William J. Terry's stuffed toys.

VOICE BOX
A prod in the tummy suggests he contains a growler, although it no longer works. It was probably the tilt variety (*see pp.14-15*).

FEET AND PAWS
Two layers of a now discolored, and slightly damaged, thin woven fabric represent foot and paw pads. This suggests that they are replacement pads or else the remains of the original lining.

Long, egg-shaped feet

Bear profile The straight, tubular body and peculiar hunchback make this bear unique.

NOSE AND MOUTH
Stitches in a green woolen thread make up the nose, and the mouth is formed using the same thin thread. This is an unusual color, so the stitches are probably the work of a repairer.

Long, silky, blond mohair plush

CLAWS
The green wool defining the claws may be repair work – the original stitching was probably black.

Long, curved, tapering arms

• BEAR ESSENTIALS •

HT: 16in (40cm)

FUR: blond, long and silky, mohair plush
EYES: large, clear, glass, pink-painted backs
EARS: small half circles, set high on head
MUZZLE: pointed with blunt tip, clipped

NOSE: hand-sewn, rectangular, green wool
ARMS: long; discolored, woven pads; claws
FEET: large; discolored, woven pads; claws
STUFFING: excelsior throughout bear

TRADEMARK: This bear does not have a trademark. William J. Terry bears often had cardboard swing tags reading "Terryer Toys"; "Marmaduke" may once have had one.

❧ "Bobby" ❧

1908 STEIFF

In 1908 Steiff introduced the Maulkorb-bär. Special features of this bear were his leather muzzle and leash, accessories inspired by dancing bears that performed in town squares of central Europe. Manufactured in brown or white, the bear was available in ten sizes. Steiff made a replica of the white muzzled bear in 1990.

EYES
"Bobby" has the small, wooden shoe button eyes commonly used by manufacturers, especially Steiff, throughout this period.

VOICE BOX
Although it is now no longer working, "Bobby" has a squeaker mechanism. It was around this time that Steiff began to use the first tilt growlers inside its bears.

ACCESSORIES
"Bobby's" muzzle is made of leather that has darkened with age. It is held together with round studs, which resemble the blank metal buttons used as trademarks on early Steiff bears. The muzzle is fastened at the back with a buckle and has a leash attached.

TRADEMARK
"Bobby" has a 1905-1950 Steiff button, bearing the name of the company.

FEET
His large feet have beige replacement felt pads. They are close in color to the original.

The small rounded ears are positioned well apart

Bear profile "Bobby's" accentuated limbs, his leather muzzle and its fastenings, and the leash, now broken, are clear from this angle.

Typical inverted V-shaped mouth hidden by muzzle

NOSE
His triangular nose is embroidered in black thread. The stitching is identical to that on "Eddie's" nose (*see p.21*).

ARMS
The long and tapering arms have curved paws with replacement beige felt pads.

CLAWS
The four claws of black thread extend across the plush section of each of the paws.

Light brown mohair plush

• BEAR ESSENTIALS •

HT: 10in (26cm)

FUR: light brown-colored, mohair plush
EYES: small, black, wooden shoe buttons
EARS: small, rounded, positioned wide apart
MUZZLE: long, protruding; leather muzzle

NOSE: hand-embroidered, triangular, black
ARMS: long, curved; beige felt pads; claws
FEET: large; beige felt pads; claws
STUFFING: excelsior throughout bear

Raised lettering

Trademark

⇒ *"Othello"* ⇐

1912 STEIFF

"Othello" belongs to a batch of black bears produced by Steiff for the British market. Available in five sizes, they were manufactured in either short or long mohair plush. Long mohair plush bears, like "Othello," are the rarest — only 494 of them were made. Steiff made one other black bear in 1907; it had red claws and a gutta-percha nose.

EARS
"Othello" has large ears, set wide apart. Like the ears of many early Steiff bears, they are sewn into the seams of his face.

Orange felt makes eyes more prominent

EYES
Each black shoe button eye is set on a circle of orange felt. This is a unique feature; the 1907 black Steiff bear had no backing for his shoe button eyes.

TRADEMARK
"Othello" has the famous Steiff "button in ear" trademark used from 1905 to 1950.

FEET
His large feet have long, narrow pads of beige felt. There are no claws stitched onto his feet and paws because the black thread normally used to match the nose would not have shown up against the bear's dark fur.

Feet in mint condition

Bear profile The long limbs, protruding muzzle, and unusual felt and shoe button eyes, are clearly defined in profile.

NOSE AND MOUTH
The hand-embroidered nose is large and rectangular. It consists of vertical black thread stitches. The stitched mouth is an inverted V shape.

ARMS
"Othello's" arms are long, tapering, and curved in the traditional manner, with pads of undamaged beige felt.

Long black mohair plush

• BEAR ESSENTIALS •

HT: 19in (48cm)

FUR: black, long, shaggy, mohair plush
EYES: medium, black, shoe buttons on felt
EARS: large, set wide apart into face seams
MUZZLE: blunt, protruding, clipped

NOSE: hand-embroidered, rectangular, black
ARMS: curved; beige felt pads; no claws
FEET: large; long, beige felt pads; no claws
STUFFING: excelsior throughout bear

Raised lettering

Trademark

THE TEDDY BEAR EXPLOSION

World War I was to have a serious effect on the toy industry in Europe, which had been a German monopoly since the nineteenth century. With borders closed and bans on German imports in most European countries, German manufacturers found business difficult. The way was open for the stuffed toy industry to develop elsewhere. The French company Thiennot made one of its first teddy bears in 1919. In Britain, several stuffed-toy firms were established during World War I, utilizing Yorkshire woven mohair plush fabric, much of which had previously been exported to Germany.

BRITISH MANUFACTURERS

The year 1914 signaled a halt to German-made teddy bears. Many factories were given over to making items for the war effort. Both partners of the newly formed Nuremberg-based Schreyer and Co. were drafted into military service, as were the three Steiff directors. In Britain, however, several toy factories were established, some for making teddy bears specifically. William Henry Jones, originally a representative for doll manufacturers in Germany, found himself jobless as a result of the war, so he turned to designing teddy bears. Other new companies dating from 1914 included the East London Federation Toy Factory, established by Sylvia Pankhurst.

TEDDY TRADE NAMES

Many of these firms had registered trade names, such as the South Wales Manufacturing Co.'s Madingland or Joseph Burman's Zoo Toy Co.'s Fondle Toys. These were rarely attached to the bear in any permanent form, creating problems for today's collectors. The Mr. Teddy cardboard swing tag of the Liverpool-based Messrs Gray & Nicholls is really only known through photographs in trade journals. Magazines such as the British *Games and Toys* or *The Toy Trader* and the American *Playthings* help greatly with research. By the 1930s, the majority of leaders of the British stuffed toy industry were all in existence, each with patented trademarks in the form of more permanent buttons or embroidered labels, a boon for today's collector. Dean's A1 and Farnell's Alpha bears were well established. By 1920,

△ **Photographic Evidence**
Photographs of still-existent bears with their original owner are popular with collectors today.

△ **Hermann's Trademark**
The 1911-1929 trademark used at the Sonneberg factory.

▽ **New Company**
The Teddy Toy Co. was founded in London in 1914.

▽ **Homemade**
A teddy made in a British home.

▽ **Hard Times**
The war years were difficult for Steiff factory workers.

△ **Chest Tag**
Ges. gesch on this trademark means "legally protected."

Chad Valley's Wrekin stuffed-toy factory in Wellington, Shropshire, had been opened, and H.G. Stone & Co. was producing its Chiltern line of teddy bears from the Chesham factory. A decade later, Merrythought had joined the ranks, the result of a partnership between textile makers W.G. Holmes and G.H. Laxton. The year 1937 saw the creation of another important teddy bear manufacturer, Pedigree Soft Toys, as well as the voluntary liquidation of W.H. Jones. This was the beginning of the end for many small businesses that were unable to cope with increasing competition and economic depression.

△ **Mascot**
The pioneering British airwoman Amy Johnson (1903-1941) with her teddy bear mascot.

NEW MATERIALS

The use of new materials changed the shape and feel of the teddy bear. Kapok was greatly preferred by many firms, not only for its softness, light weight, and cleanliness, but also because it could be bought cheaply from countries within the British Empire. Teddy bears with coats of artificial silk plush, woven from fibers consisting of reconstituted cellulose from woody plants, were introduced, often dyed in a range of colors. As early as 1919, the Wholesale Toy Co. was offering a pink teddy bear.

WORLD WAR II

The coming of World War II had a dramatic effect on the manufacture of the teddy bear. Hitler's rise to power in 1933 left many German toy companies and export houses in disarray. In Britain, Farnell's factory was bombed during the London blitz, while output in many companies was gradually turned over to essential supplies. Dean's made life jackets and Merrythought made helmet linings, hot water bottle covers, and gas mask cases. Some companies, including Chad Valley, were allowed to produce a limited toy quota. Rather touchingly, its 1942 advertisement featured a teddy bear with the words, "Though his fur is shorter and his stuffing less silky than in times of peace, the same care goes into his production...."

△ **Collector in the Making**
Plummy is photographed here with his young owner, who was later to collect and restore teddy bears for a living.

▷ **A1 Toys**
The trademark for Dean's Rag Book Co. in the 1920s.

△ **H.G. Stone's Trademark**
"Chiltern" refers to the site of the factory.

▽ **Wartime Evacuees**
Teddy bears were a great source of comfort to the children who were evacuated from England during World War II.

△ **Postcards**
Teddy bear postcards have always been popular with collectors.

BEAR NECESSITIES

As the teddy bear evolved, his limbs grew shorter, his body fatter, and his muzzle less pronounced. Synthetic plush fabrics such as rayon and nylon were introduced, glass eyes became the norm, and kapok stuffing was used for the entire body, producing a more cuddly toy. During both World Wars, no mohair plush was available and kapok was in short supply, so substitutes had to be found.

Glass eyes with wire shanks

Shoe buttons

Clear glass eye

Glass eyes on wire hooks

Wired glass eyes

EYES
Shoe buttons were used until the early 1920s, although Steiff went over to glass completely in 1921; glass eyes were held on short wire hooks or long wire shanks.

c. 1930 BRITISH
This bear has glass eyes, velveteen pads, and kapok stuffing – new developments in teddy design – but still has mohair plush.

WOOL AND THREAD
During World War II, rationing of raw materials kept teddy bears in short supply, while parents resorted to knitting soft toys from unraveled wool.

1930s woven silk mohair plush

FABRIC
Woven mohair plush continued to be popular, but the invention of man-made fibers revolutionized the stuffed toy industry. In the 1920s artificial silk plush (rayon) was made; the first completely synthetic fiber, nylon, was invented in 1938.

Woven mohair plush

Woven mohair and synthetic plush

Woven nylon and acrylic plush

Sheepskin

Artificial silk plush (rayon)

JOINTS
The combination of metal and cardboard disks inside the jointing system of some bears remained unchanged (*see p.14*).

Embroidery thread

Thread for machine-stitching

Cardboard

Felt

Velveteen

Woven cotton

Rexine

PAW AND FOOT PADS

Cardboard was used in the earlier period for reinforcing the feet, but it was especially typical of 1920s and 1930s teddy bears. Claws (as well as noses and mouths) were sewn with embroidery thread.

FELT AND FABRIC PADS

Throughout this period, pads were made from felt, although other materials were used as well. Velveteen (a short-pile cotton fabric) and brushed cotton fabrics, and Rexine, the trade name for a kind of treated muslin or oilcloth used by English manufacturers starting in about 1930, were all popular.

Squeaker

Interior of tilt growler

SQUEAKER

The oval cardboard and oilcloth squeakers were still used in teddy bears throughout this period.

1920s TILT GROWLER

Tilt growlers with weighted, hinged bellows were used until the 1920s, although their cardboard canisters became slightly more sophisticated – the lids were made from perforated cardboard instead of gauze.

Tilt growler showing perforated cardboard lid

Porcelain weight

Tilt growler mechanism

Oilcloth bellows

Kapok

1930s TILT GROWLER

In the new tilt growler of the 1930s, a porcelain weight operated the bellows, forcing air over the reed and through a waxed paper membrane.

Excelsior

STUFFING

Although excelsior was still used, kapok soon became popular for stuffing the entire bear, following its success as a filling in life jackets during World War I. Its hollow, silky fibers resisted vermin, insects, and bacteria, making it clean, light, and cuddly. After 1939, kapok was in short supply, so a substitute called sub, art wool, or flock, was developed from the waste material of textile mills.

Sub and excelsior

Inside of music box

Music box lid

Music box

MUSIC BOXES

By the 1930s, many bears contained music boxes operated on the Swiss comb and toothed-cylinder principle: once wound up, a canister turned, letting the tuned teeth of a comb strike the pins and produce a tune. Brahms' *Lullaby* and *The Teddy Bears Picnic* were common tunes.

Sub

BEAR APPAREL

With the introduction of newspaper comic strips and cartoon characters in the movies, stuffed toy manufacturers turned from producing naturalistic animals to caricatured cats, dogs, rabbits, and teddy bears; the outfits on some of these soft toys were as humorous as their expressions. During the 1920s and 1930s, some teddy bears were made with their clothes and bodies all in one piece, so that they could not be undressed. For undressed bears, popular sources of teddy outfits were the knitting patterns that appeared in the ever-increasing numbers of women's magazines. During the two World Wars, teddy bears became patriotic mascots dressed in military uniforms.

TEDDY CLOWNS

During the 1920s and 1930s, there was a tremendous demand for dressed bears in the United States. Steiff produced a number of bears in costume especially for the American market. An example was the white, blond, or dark brown plush Teddybu. He was made in four sizes from 1925 to 1927; the bear wore a felt vest with three buttons. The company's Teddy Clown of 1926-28 came in eleven sizes in pink, gold, or brown-tipped mohair plush, complete with ruff and pierrot hat. Bears in clown outfits had been available in the United States since about 1907 and owed their popularity to the appearance of teddy clowns in Seymour Eaton's Roosevelt Bear books. Clown suits often formed part of the complete teddy bear trousseaus available during the 1930s. These trousseaus consisted of a trunk of outfits, including, for example, an Indian, a cowboy, a Tyrolean, and ski togs.

△ **Going Dutch**
In the 1930s Dutch trousers were popular.

◁ **Trilbies**
During this period, some teddy bears were dressed in salesmen's samples, such as trilbies.

△ **Page Boy**
This Chiltern teddy bear's page boy uniform is all-in-one with the body. Made in the 1930s, it was also available in pink plush.

▷ **Homemade Outfit**
The outfit and scarlet tam o'shanter were lovingly knitted by the bear's seven-year-old English owner in 1944. Many other wartime teds were given similar clothes.

▷ **Gas Mask**
A gas mask for a teddy bear made from tin and oilcloth.

Δ 1930s Bare Bears
*Bears designed to be clothed were
made with no hair on their bodies.*

WARTIME TEDS

The outbreak of World War I inspired a number of patriotic
mascots, including the teddy bear. It became the fashion to dress
teddy bears in uniforms identical to that of a father, husband,
brother, or sweetheart who had gone to the front. Many people
made their own uniforms – some are still worn by the soldier and
sailor bears on display at Pollock's Toy Museum and the Bethnal
Green Museum of Childhood, respectively, in London. Teddy bears
dressed in Russian clothes were particulary popular. In 1915, for
example, the London Toy Co. designed Ivan, the Russian Tommy.

ALLY BEARS

A few uniforms were made commercially. The most famous are
worn by the Ally Bears, a charming collection of teddy bears
dressed in the various uniforms of the allied forces. They were
made by the London firm Harwin and Co. starting in 1915. The
Ally Bears were designed by the director's daughter, Dorothy
Harwin, and they include a British sailor and admiral, a Red
Cross nurse, and various soldiers, including a Scot wearing a
kilt, sporran, and spats, and an Australian wearing a turned-
up, wide-brimmed hat tilted across one ear. Ally Bears are
rarely found intact today, although you can see one at the
Museum of Childhood, Sudbury Hall, England.

Δ Regimental Dress
*During World War II, this 1905 Steiff bear was
outfitted in the uniform of the Scottish regiment,
the Black Watch.*

▷ Master Teddy
*This 1915 teddy with his typical
googly eyes was produced by the
Chiltern Toy Works of Chesham,
England, later to become H.G.
Stone & Co. Ltd.*

BEAR MEMORABILIA

The years between the two World Wars saw a continuing demand for teddy bear novelties. Numerous clockwork bears were produced by the major manufacturers, although they are hard for collectors to identify because they are often similar, and many do not have trademarks. Miniature Schuco bears produced in various colors were very popular. Musical bears dressed as clowns or in other costumes were made in the United States and Europe, and the teddy bear acquired his own theme tune when, in 1930, songwriter Jimmy Kennedy added lyrics to the melody for The Teddy Bears Picnic.

△ **Two-faced Bear**
A 1930s Schuco bear.

△ **Clockwork**
A 1915 Steiff bear who somersaults.

NEW TEDDY BEAR DESIGNS
In the UK, the banning of the sale of German goods during World War I, and the subsequent rise of the British stuffed toy industry, resulted in the introduction of various innovations to the basic teddy bear design. In 1916, the British Doll and Novelty Co. made the teddy bear exerciser for children: the action of fully extending the bear's spring-loaded arms was considered beneficial to a child's muscles. In 1918, Messrs Isaacs and Co. made the Spring Leg Teddy Bear with long legs and boots equipped with patented Isa springs that were activated when the child pulled the leash. A series of kapok-stuffed, mohair plush toys called Bendy Bears were made by Dean's in the early 1920s. Each had an internal metal framework that allowed the bear to be manipulated. H.G. Stone copied the Schuco-style bears with nodding heads. Its own Wagmee series was introduced in the late 1930s, and Steiff developed similar bears.

▽ **Compact Bear**
A compact made in the 1930s by Schuco. It had a mirror, a powder container, and a central stem to hold lipstick. Other Schuco bears were made to hold perfume.

◁ **Two-tone Bear**
This bear's fur is dyed to make him resemble a clown. Two-tone bears were especially popular.

▷ **Skating Bear**
The Bing Skating Bear dates from 1915. The firm's metal tag trademark is in his right ear.

CLOCKWORK BEARS

The clockwork bears of this period are especially interesting, and if in working order, they fetch high prices in today's market. Collectors should especially watch for Gebrüder Bing's Walking Bear of c. 1915. It had a large key in its belly that operated its mechanism. Bing also produced tumbling bears, as did Steiff and Schuco. Bing and Schuco made skating bears that may have been inspired by Alice Teddy, a real bear that roller-skated in the United States before World War I. The Schuco Skating Bear wore a felt uniform and cap; his large metal feet had wheels attached to them. In the mid-1920s, Steiff made its Urteddy. This was similar to the earlier wheeled teddy (see pp.18-19), but he also had a clockwork mechanism attached to the chassis. Other wheeled bears, including Teddy Baby (see p.49) and Baby Bear, who lay appealingly on his back with bells on his paws, were produced. From the 1920s and 1930s on, the teddy bear was developed as a container. Steiff was the first to do this with its unique teddy-shaped purses and tea cozies. In London, J. and A.J. Burman made its Teddy to-T, a teddy bear with an empty stomach that could be used as a small case.

△ 1930s Record
The Teddy Bears Picnic

◁ Pillbox Hat
This felt pillbox hat is slightly worn, although the leather strap is in good shape.

△ Bag
This Schuco bear still has a leather bag on a strap slung across his chest. It is unusual to find this particular Schuco bear with his accessories intact.

△ Gas Mask and Case
A gas mask case with a plush teddy bear in felt clothing on its side. This was designed to comfort an English child during World War II.

◁ Bellhop Bear
A Schuco bear dating from 1923. He is fully jointed and wears the snappy felt livery of a hotel bellhop. The bear's tail operates his moving head. He also has a squeaker inside his chest. He is very rare, made more valuable by the fact that he is in mint condition and he retains his trademark.

"Louise"

1921 STEIFF

During World War I, the Steiff factory produced only war supplies, including ammunition, airplane parts, and gas masks for horses. After the war, however, the introduction of a conveyor belt system in 1921 improved efficiency, and the factory was soon on its feet again, producing bears like "Louise."

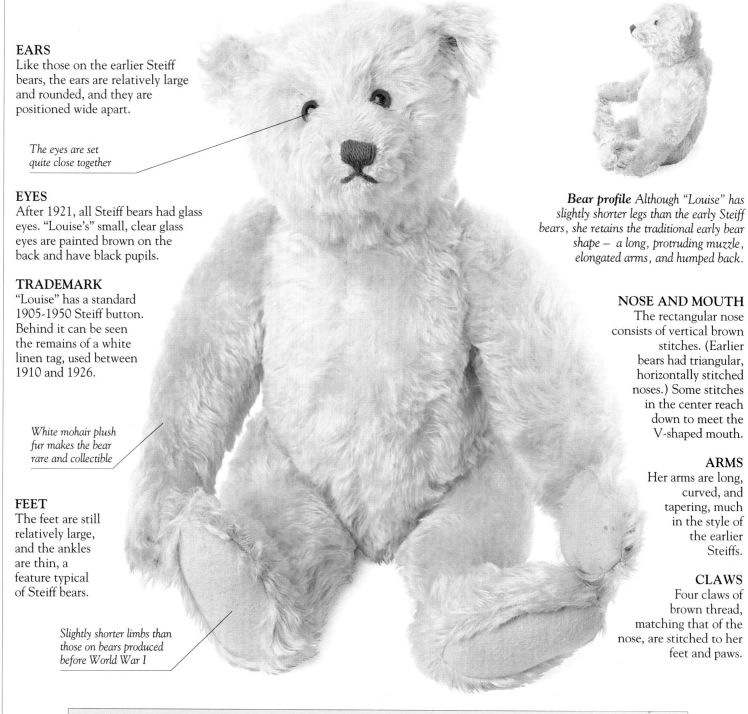

EARS
Like those on the earlier Steiff bears, the ears are relatively large and rounded, and they are positioned wide apart.

The eyes are set quite close together

EYES
After 1921, all Steiff bears had glass eyes. "Louise's" small, clear glass eyes are painted brown on the back and have black pupils.

TRADEMARK
"Louise" has a standard 1905-1950 Steiff button. Behind it can be seen the remains of a white linen tag, used between 1910 and 1926.

White mohair plush fur makes the bear rare and collectible

FEET
The feet are still relatively large, and the ankles are thin, a feature typical of Steiff bears.

Slightly shorter limbs than those on bears produced before World War I

Bear profile *Although "Louise" has slightly shorter legs than the early Steiff bears, she retains the traditional early bear shape – a long, protruding muzzle, elongated arms, and humped back.*

NOSE AND MOUTH
The rectangular nose consists of vertical brown stitches. (Earlier bears had triangular, horizontally stitched noses.) Some stitches in the center reach down to meet the V-shaped mouth.

ARMS
Her arms are long, curved, and tapering, much in the style of the earlier Steiffs.

CLAWS
Four claws of brown thread, matching that of the nose, are stitched to her feet and paws.

• BEAR ESSENTIALS •

HT: 15in (39cm)

FUR: white, shaggy, mohair plush
EYES: small, clear glass, brown-painted backs
EARS: large, rounded, placed wide apart
MUZZLE: slightly raised, protruding

NOSE: hand-embroidered, rectangular, brown
ARMS: long, curved; cream felt pads; claws
FEET: large; long, cream felt pads; claws
STUFFING: excelsior and kapok mixture

Raised lettering

Trademark

❧ "Mr. Fluffy" ❧
1923 CHAD VALLEY

This bear was manufactured at the Wrekin factory in Wellington, Shropshire, by the British toy company Chad Valley. The firm began to specialize in stuffed toys in 1920. "Mr. Fluffy" is one of its earliest teddy bears carrying the Aerolite trademark, an indication that kapok was used as a stuffing.

EYES
His rich amber eyes with black pupils are made from glass and are held on wire shanks. They are stitched into place.

VOICE BOX
The round, squeaker-type voice box, which can be felt at the front of the body, no longer works.

STUFFING
Aerolite is the trade name for the kapok stuffing used in bears of this period. While the limbs of this bear are filled with kapok, his head and body are probably a mixture of kapok and the more compact excelsior.

TRADEMARK
The small metal button has an off-white celluloid center bearing the Aerolite trademark. The button, used by Chad Valley between 1923 and 1926, was intended to imitate Steiff's mark of excellence without violating the patent.

Thick cardboard reinforces the velveteen pads

FEET
The soles are more oval than those found on the feet of the earlier Steiffs.

Large flat ears on the sides of the head

Bear profile *The round, protruding forehead and prominent but blunt muzzle, the less accentuated humpback and shorter limbs all reveal the emergence of a new teddy bear shape.*

NOSE AND MOUTH
The triangular nose consists mainly of vertical stitches, with a few horizontal stitches along the top. Originally, the nose was black, but some of the outermost stitches have become discolored with age. The inverted, V-shaped mouth curls upward slightly to form an endearing smile.

Four black stitched claws on each paw

FUR
A long-pile golden mohair was used for most of the bear. The mohair on his muzzle is clipped.

The arms are slightly shorter than those of the early bears

There are five claws on each foot

• BEAR ESSENTIALS •

FUR: golden, long, silky, mohair plush
EYES: medium, amber, glass, black pupils
EARS: large, flat, placed on sides of head
MUZZLE: blunt, protruding, clipped plush
HT: 16in (40cm)

NOSE: hand-embroidered, triangular, black
ARMS: curved; brown velveteen pads; claws
FEET: large; brown velveteen pads; claws
STUFFING: excelsior and kapok mixture

Aerolite mark

Trademark

❧ Peter ❧

1925 GEBRUDER SUSSENGUTH

Peter was the creation of the Süssenguth factory in Neustadt-bei-Coburg, Germany, which had manufactured and exported dolls and toys since 1894. Few of these bears were sold at the time because, it is said, the bear's rolling eyes and bared teeth frightened children. Consequently, this bear is now rare.

HEAD
Peter's head, with its chubby cheeks, is made of a molded, hard, plasterlike material called "composition." The material is so named because it is "composed" of a variety of substances, including plaster, sawdust, and rags.

Black-outlined sockets

EYES
Peter's googly eyes are made of white and black glass. Set in round sockets cut into the face, they are attached to his tongue inside his head. When Peter is tilted, his tongue moves from side to side, and his eyes roll from left to right.

FUR
This particular Peter is made from beige mohair plush, tipped with dark brown. He was also produced in gray tipped with black, as well as gold plush. Bears made in gold plush are the most unusual.

STUFFING
While his body and limbs are stuffed with excelsior, the molded composition head is hollow.

Hollow head contains movable eyes and tongue

Bear profile *From the side, you can see Peter's long, straight back and his open mouth with a moving, protruding tongue.*

White composition visible beneath peeling black paint

NOSE
The nose is molded to have two nostrils. It extends from beneath the plush and is part of the hollow composition head.

MOUTH
Peter's open mouth reveals molded teeth outlined in red paint. He even has two extended canines in the top jaw, and these are made from the same material as his head and nose. The movable tongue, a thin pointed piece of composition, is pale pink.

Notice the absence of claws on the feet

• BEAR ESSENTIALS •

HT: 14in (35cm)

FUR: brown-tipped, beige, dual mohair plush
EYES: large, white and black, glass, deep-set
EARS: small, round, set toward back of head
MUZZLE: pointed; open, molded mouth

NOSE: molded composition, square, black
ARMS: long; flesh-colored, felt pads; no claws
FEET: long; flesh-colored, felt pads; no claws
STUFFING: composition and excelsior

TRADEMARK: A printed, round, cardboard swing tag is often attached to Peter's chest reading "Peter Ges. Gesch. Nr 895257." This tag is legally protected.

❧ "Happy" ☙

1926 STEIFF

In 1989, "Happy Anniversary" was sold at Sotheby's in London for $86,350 and she still holds the record for being the most expensive teddy bear bought at auction. The new owner presented the bear to his wife as a wedding anniversary present. All three now live in California.

EARS
The large rounded ears are set wide apart and sit on the sides, rather than the top, of her head. Their positioning is very similar to that on some of the earlier Steiff bears, like "Friend Petz" *(see p.23).*

Her large brown glass eyes have black pupils

EYES
"Happy" has brown glass eyes. She was possibly designed as a prototype for the Petsy bear registered in 1927. Petsy had brown or blue glass eyes. The bears with blue eyes are more collectible.

VOICE BOX
"Happy" has a squeaker mechanism, although it no longer works.

FEET
Her large feet with narrow pads are pre-World War I style.

Bear profile *Notice her long limbs, humped back, and large head with protruding muzzle.*

NOSE
Hand-embroidered in brown thread, her nose matches the color of the dual plush. It is large, heart-shaped, and consists of vertical stitches.

Long, tapering arms end in curved paws

FUR
Her attractive, dual mohair plush was extremely popular in the 1920s.

Large, spoonlike pads in the style of early German bears

• BEAR ESSENTIALS •

HT: 24in (62cm)

FUR: brown-tipped beige, dual mohair plush
EYES: large, brown, glass with black pupils
EARS: large, round, wide apart, side of head
MUZZLE: long, blunt, and protruding

NOSE : hand-embroidered, heart-shaped, brown
ARMS: long, tapering; beige felt pads; claws
FEET: large, narrow; beige felt pads; no claws
STUFFING: excelsior throughout bear

Raised lettering

Trademark

❧ "Claus" ❧

1927 GEBRUDER HERMANN

"Claus" is a product of one of Steiff's German rivals, the Gebrüder Hermann factory, founded in 1907. "Claus" was made in Sonneberg, then the center of the toy-making industry. Steiff and Hermann bears can be difficult to tell apart, although the muzzle on a Hermann is usually made of a different material from the rest of his body.

Slightly gathered ears

EARS
Two semicircles of cloth form each ear. The back of the ear is made from the dual plush used for the rest of the body, while the front has the same short-pile mohair that covers the muzzle. The ears are placed centrally across the top of the two facial seams.

EYES
The bear's glass eyes are brown with black pupils.

Both the nose and mouth are embroidered with black thread

NOSE AND MOUTH
His nose is portrayed with horizontal stitches and the mouth has a gentle upward curve.

STUFFING
The head, limbs, and body of this bear are all filled with excelsior.

FEET
The clearly defined feet are quite small, and they have oval cream felt pads.

Bear profile "Claus" has a *straighter back and less rounded head than Steiff examples.*

ARMS
The arms are characteristic of those on early bears – long, curved, and slightly tapering, with pads of cream-colored felt.

Black thread claws stitched onto the plush parts of the paws

FUR
The main body is made of dual-colored mohair plush: beige, tipped with rich cinnamon. This plush was a popular material in the 1920s. On the muzzle (and fronts of the ears) a short-pile cream mohair plush is used.

• BEAR ESSENTIALS •

HT: 17in (42cm)

FUR: cinnamon-tipped beige, mohair plush
EYES: small, brown, glass, black pupils
EARS: small, semicircles, over face seams
MUZZLE: thin, cream, short, mohair plush

NOSE: hand-embroidered, rectangular, black
ARMS: small; cream felt pads; black claws
FEET: small; cream felt pads; claws
STUFFING: excelsior throughout bear

TRADEMARK: The Hermann trademark found on this bear is a round metal swing tag attached to a red cord, which is fastened to his chest.

❧ "Gloria's Bear" ❧

1920s SCHREYER & CO.

Originally owned by a child who died in the 1920s, this tiny bear still lives with a small celluloid doll in the little girl's doll house, "Cliftonville" (now in a London museum). He is a particularly early example of the Schuco mascot bears, produced by the Nuremberg-based company established in 1912.

EARS
His ears are made from tiny half circles of cardboard, covered with mohair plush. They are inserted into the seams along the top of the bear's head.

EYES
Black glass beads, probably on wire shanks, are used as eyes. These were common in small bears of the 1920s.

TRADEMARK
The Schuco trademark was formed from the first letters of the three words making up the company's German name: Schreyer und Co (Sch-u-co). Miniature bears were the company's specialty – in the 1920s, the average size of these bears was 2¹⁄₂ inches.

Felt stuck to the end of the metal arm

PAWS
Made out of hand-shaped pieces of felt, the paws are a unique feature. Later Schuco bears had more conventional paws and feet, so these felt ones indicate a bear made between 1920 and 1930.

FEET
Small V-shaped metal slivers jut out from the ends of his legs and are covered with beige felt to form the feet.

Beige felt paws

Muzzle occupies most of the bear's face

Bear profile *From this angle, you can see the bear's straight limbs and large head.*

NOSE AND MOUTH
Horizontal stitches of black thread, shaped into a triangle, indicate his nose. The bear's mouth is also stitched.

Short, dense mohair plush is ideal for a small bear

ARMS AND LEGS
The arms and legs are straight. They are jointed using metal pins that pass through the top and bottom of the body. The flat-headed ends of the pins are just visible in the center of the thigh and on the bear's upper arm.

STUFFING
"Gloria's Bear" is not stuffed in the usual way. A metal frame is covered with mohair plush, partly sewn and partly glued in place. This makes him feel very solid.

Felt has worn away on his feet, revealing the metal frame beneath

---

• BEAR ESSENTIALS •

HT: 2¹⁄₂in (6cm)

FUR: golden, short-pile, mohair plush
EYES: small, black, glass beads
EARS: tiny, half circles, along top of head
MUZZLE: blunt, protruding

NOSE: hand-embroidered, triangular, black
ARMS: straight; beige felt on paws; no claws
FEET: small; beige felt pads; no claws
STUFFING: internal metal frame

DISTINGUISHING FEATURES: The diminutive stature, metal frame, and unique felt paws are the most distinctive features of this tiny bear.

❧ *"Bertie"* ❧

1930 DEAN'S RAG BOOK CO.

This bear was made by Britain's oldest existing stuffed toy manufacturer. Founded in 1903 and originally famous for its printed cloth cut-out sheets of toys, Dean's began to make traditional jointed plush teddy bears in about 1915. "Bertie" was created at the height of its success.

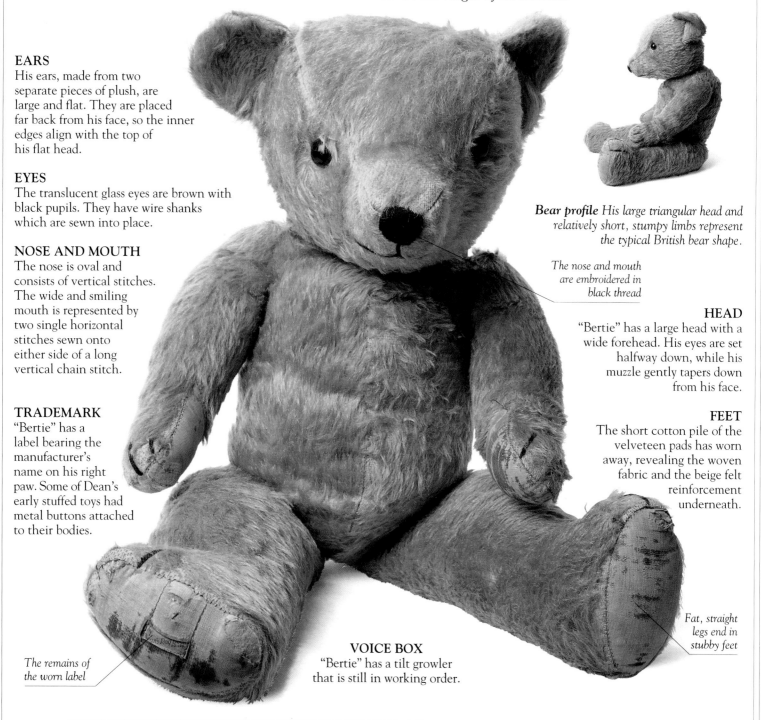

EARS
His ears, made from two separate pieces of plush, are large and flat. They are placed far back from his face, so the inner edges align with the top of his flat head.

EYES
The translucent glass eyes are brown with black pupils. They have wire shanks which are sewn into place.

NOSE AND MOUTH
The nose is oval and consists of vertical stitches. The wide and smiling mouth is represented by two single horizontal stitches sewn onto either side of a long vertical chain stitch.

TRADEMARK
"Bertie" has a label bearing the manufacturer's name on his right paw. Some of Dean's early stuffed toys had metal buttons attached to their bodies.

The remains of the worn label

Bear profile *His large triangular head and relatively short, stumpy limbs represent the typical British bear shape.*

The nose and mouth are embroidered in black thread

HEAD
"Bertie" has a large head with a wide forehead. His eyes are set halfway down, while his muzzle gently tapers down from his face.

FEET
The short cotton pile of the velveteen pads has worn away, revealing the woven fabric and the beige felt reinforcement underneath.

Fat, straight legs end in stubby feet

VOICE BOX
"Bertie" has a tilt growler that is still in working order.

• BEAR ESSENTIALS •

HT: 26in (65cm)

FUR: dark beige, soft, short, mohair plush
EYES: small, translucent, brown, glass
EARS: large, flat, set back and wide apart
MUZZLE: blunt, gently tapers from head

NOSE: hand-embroidered, oval, black
ARMS: stumpy; beige velveteen pads; claws
FEET: stumpy; beige velveteen pads; claws
STUFFING: excelsior, kapok, mix of both

MADE IN ENGLAND by Dean's Rag Book CO. LTD. LONDON

Trademark

❧ Teddy Baby ❧

1930 STEIFF

Originally designed in 1929 but rejected by the Patent Office, Steiff's successful Teddy Baby series was finally accepted the following year. He was advertised as a "life-like comical, young bear-cub, whose friendly face speaks volumes," and he was produced in different sizes, materials, and colors. He remained popular into the 1950s.

EARS
Teddy Baby has small stiff ears, although his right one has collapsed a little with time.

EYES
His brown glass eyes with black pupils have wire shanks and are set in the seam that joins the clipped mohair muzzle to the main part of his head.

VOICE BOX
A large oval squeaker about four inches long can be felt inside Teddy Baby's long, fat tummy. Still working, it sounds more like a duck than a bear cub.

A printed swing tag and bell are attached to his collar

FUR
The main body of this Teddy Baby is covered in an attractive peach cotton plush. (His muzzle is clipped mohair plush.) Other materials used for the production of this particular line included wool mohair and artificial silk plush in colors such as white, beige, dark brown, and an unusual blue.

Teddy Baby's large flat feet resemble clowns' shoes

FEET
His feet are made of the same short white mohair plush as his muzzle. The woven pink cotton pads are reinforced with cardboard.

Steiff button

Bear profile *The unusually curved, S-shaped arms, particularly flat feet, protruding muzzle, and open mouth give him a distinctive profile.*

Blue leatherette collar fastened at the back of the neck with a metal button

NOSE
The brown vertical stitches are short on the outer edge, but become longer toward the center, extending down to the top of the jaw.

MOUTH
The open mouth of this particular Teddy Baby reveals a flesh-colored felt palate. His chin is covered with clipped mohair plush in cream, and the muzzle is of the same material in white. A few Teddy Babies were produced with closed mouths.

ACCESSORIES
Some bears were made with collars, a few had ribbon bows – and others wore nothing at all. Certain early versions were dressed in pink dresses and shoes, and lace-trimmed bibs.

• BEAR ESSENTIALS •

HT: 12in (30cm)

FUR: peach cotton plush; clipped mohair
EYES: medium, brown, glass, black pupils
EARS: small, curved, stiff and set upright
MUZZLE: protruding, open mouth, clipped

NOSE: hand-embroidered, heart-shaped, brown
ARMS: tapering; pink cotton pads; claws
FEET: large, flat; pink cotton pads; claws
STUFFING: excelsior throughout bear

Trademark

RUPERT BEAR

In November 1920, the Daily Express, *an English newspaper, introduced Rupert Bear. By the time the Rupert League was formed in 1932, Rupert had become a national institution. The League's aims were "… to be cheerful, unselfish and to strive … to make people happy." His appeal was universal, and soon he became known in some twenty different countries. Rupert Bear memorabilia was produced, and he was used often as a mascot for fund-raising campaigns.*

△ **Mary Tourtel**
The creator of Rupert.

RUPERT'S ADVENTURES

Rupert Bear was the creation of Mary Tourtel, a children's book illustrator. Mary's husband, an editor on the *Daily Express*, had been looking for a comic strip to rival those of other national newspapers. Rupert Bear ended the search. Mary Tourtel set her stories in an idyllic, timeless town called Nutwood, where Rupert usually became involved in fairy tale adventures featuring witches, ogres, and dragons. He also had a set of lovable and imaginatively named friends: Bill Badger, Algy Pug, Edward Trunk, and the Wise Old Goat.

A CONTINUING TRADITION

In 1935, Mary Tourtel retired because of failing sight, but her work was continued by the magazine and book illustrator Alfred Bestall. He drew the daily adventures in the newspaper for the next 30 years, and also, from 1936, the annual Rupert comic books. From 1965 to 1978, the cartoon animator Alex Cubie illustrated Rupert's adventures; Freddie Chaplain wrote the stories. Today Rupert is illustrated by John Harrold and written by Ian Robinson.

∇ **Annuals**
Two Rupert Daily Express annuals, dating from 1949 (left), and 1952 (right).

◁ **Marionette**
A Rupert marionette made in the late 1950s by Pelham Puppets. Like the original drawings of Rupert, this bear has human hands.

∇ **Dutch Version**
Since the 1920s, Rupert has been popular in Holland. This set of four postcards and envelope, illustrated by Mary Tourtel, is very rare. They make up one of two series published in the mid-1920s. In Holland, Rupert was known as Bruintje Beer (Brown Bear) and his adventures appeared in the Dutch newspaper Algameen Handelsblad.

▷ **Pop-up Bear**
*Rupert Bear appeared
in pop-up annuals
published by the
Daily Express.
This 1931 annual
shows Rupert in
original clothes:
a blue sweater,
gray check
trousers,
and scarf.*

BIRTH OF AN INDUSTRY

The first Rupert merchandise was the Little Bear
Embroidery Card made in 1921. Two years later a
play was produced based on Rupert's adventures. It
was called *Rupert's Revenge* and was written for the
Daily Express Women's Exhibition in London.
Starting in the 1960s, numerous toys (including a
talking version by Pedigree Soft Toys and a rubber
Bendy Toy by Newfeld Ltd.), puppets, board games,
jigsaws, and money boxes were made. Rupert's appearance in
two cartoon series, shown on television in the 1970s and
1980s, and a video in 1984, increased his commerical appeal.
In 1983, an organization, The Followers of Rupert, was founded
to maintain the purity of the Rupert tradition. Its 700 members
throughout the world receive the journal, *Nutwood*, twice a year.
A collection of Rupert Bear artifacts is housed in the local
museum of Mary Tourtel's hometown, Canterbury, England.

▽ **1986 Rupert Bear**
A Real Soft Toys design.

△ **Rupert and the Frog Chorus**
*A still from the 1984 cartoon made by animator Geoff
Dunbar and musician Paul McCartney.*

◁ **Recording Artist**
*A record produced by BBC television to celebrate
the 50th anniversary of the Rupert Bear annuals.*

❧ "Compton" ❧
1920s J.K. FARNELL

This bear's general shape and unusual claw markings suggest that he was probably manufactured by J.K. Farnell (Est.1897), one of Britain's oldest stuffed toy companies. The absence of any trademarks, however, makes positive identification of "Compton" difficult.

EARS
"Compton's" small ears sit wide apart at a slightly jaunty angle. The inner edges are sewn into his facial seams, while the outer edges align with the sides of his head.

EYES
The clear glass eyes, with painted backs, give "Compton" a wide-eyed, surprised look. They are on wire shanks, sewn into his face with strong thread.

CLAWS
The design for the bear's claws was used by W.J. Terry before 1920 and by Merrythought after 1930.

STUFFING
"Compton" is mainly stuffed with kapok, but he has some excelsior in his muzzle and also around his joints.

Clipped muzzle

***Bear profile** This angle emphasizes the likeness between Farnell bears and Steiff bears, especially "Maximilian" (see p.24): the protruding muzzle, humped back, long limbs.*

NOSE AND MOUTH
His nose is embroidered with vertical black thread stitches; the outer stitches are extra long, extending over the upper edge of the bear's slightly lopsided nose. His mouth is an inverted V with stitching joining it to the nose.

ARMS
The long, tapering arms are like those seen on early Steiff bears. They curve upward at the point where the paws start.

Joined claws are stitched across his felt pads

Long narrow feet

Spoonlike pads of beige felt

• BEAR ESSENTIALS •

HT: 16in (40cm)

FUR: golden, slightly shaggy, mohair plush
EYES: medium, clear glass, painted backs
EARS: small, set wide apart
MUZZLE: blunt, protruding, clipped short

NOSE: hand-embroidered, lopsided, black
ARMS: long, curved; beige felt pads; claws
FEET: large, narrow; beige felt pads; claws
STUFFING: excelsior and kapok mixture

DISTINGUISHING FEATURES:
"Compton's" unusual joined claws, indicated with black thread and stitched across the beige felt pads, make him easily recognizable.

❧ *"Chummy"* ❧

1930-1935 MERRYTHOUGHT LTD.

"Chummy" is one of the earliest bears produced by Merrythought which, in 1930, began manufacturing stuffed toys in Ironbridge, Shropshire, England. Chad Valley's factory was not far away, and over the next ten years both companies produced similar cuddly, kapok-filled bears. Sometimes the bears are difficult to tell apart.

EARS
"Chummy" has large, flat, rounded ears similar to Chad Valley's "Mr. Fluffy" *(see p.43)*. Set quite far back, they are placed across the seams of his face.

EYES
The amber glass eyes with black pupils are on wire shanks, sewn into place through the seams of his face. They are set so low down that they accentuate "Chummy's" large forehead.

Golden mohair plush

STUFFING
Like most British bears of this period, "Chummy" is stuffed with a kapok and excelsior mix; his limbs are all kapok.

FEET
The feet are small and the ankles are thin compared with the fat thighs. The foot pads on "Chummy" are felt, although Merrythought occasionally used brown velveteen on these bears.

Pointed, clipped muzzle

Bear profile *Notice "Chummy's" arms and the absence of a hump on his back – characteristics that distinguish the new-style British bear from early German bears.*

TRADEMARK
A celluloid button anchored in his left ear shows a wishbone; Merrythought is an old English word for wishbone.

VOICE BOX
"Chummy's" voice box no longer works.

CLAWS
The claws are typical of Merrythought bears of the period. Four are stitched across each felt pad, then their inner ends are joined with horizontal stitches.

A well-matched replacement felt pad

Joined claws

• BEAR ESSENTIALS •

HT: 23in (57cm)

FUR: golden, slightly shaggy, mohair plush
EYES: large, amber, glass, black pupils
EARS: large, flat, high on back of head
MUZZLE: pointed, facing down, clipped

NOSE: hand-embroidered, rectangular
ARMS: long, curved; rust felt pads; claws
FEET: medium; rust felt pads; claws
STUFFING: kapok, excelsior/kapok

MERRYTHOUGHT HYGIENIC TOYS MADE IN ENGLAND

Trademark

❧ "Colin" ❧

1930-1935 MERRYTHOUGHT LTD.

"Colin" is part of the Magnet Line, the first series of teddy bears produced by the British company Merrythought in the early 1930s. Like the previous Merrythought bear (see p.53), he has a celluloid button, although this is attached to his back and not to his left ear. The firm was forced to move the button because it copied Steiff's "button in ear."

EARS
His ears are small, rounded, and placed wide apart, giving him an astonished appearance. The inner edges are just caught into his facial seams, like the ears on Dean's "Bertie" (*see p.48*).

The bulbous eyes are typical of a Merrythought bear

EYES
The eyes are a rich, dark amber glass with black pupils. The wire shanks are inserted into the seams of the bear's face and sewn into place.

VOICE BOX
"Colin" has a squeaker-type voice box, similar to the one found in Merrythought's "Chummy" (*see p.53*).

Golden mohair plush

CLAWS
Five unjoined claws are embroidered on each front paw. Four claws are stitched on each foot.

FEET
His feet are small, with short and narrow, oval pads of beige, woven, brushed cotton.

Bear profile This view accentuates Colin's triangular head with his upward-pointing muzzle. The upper paws look thin, and his thighs appear to merge into his ankles and feet.

Pointed, clipped muzzle

NOSE AND MOUTH
"Colin" has an oblong nose of vertical stitches across the end seam of his muzzle. His mouth consists of two sets of double stitches. The thread appears brown, but may be a discolored black.

ARMS
The arms are short, reaching down only to the tops of his thighs.

The paws are particularly narrow

TRADEMARK
"Colin" has a woven label on his left foot. Like "Chummy," he also has a yellow celluloid button on his back, behind his left arm joint.

• BEAR ESSENTIALS •

HT: 20in (50cm)

FUR: golden, threadbare mohair plush
EYES: bulbous, dark amber, glass, black pupils
EARS: small, erect, set wide apart in face seams
MUZZLE: pointed, turning upward, clipped

NOSE: hand-embroidered, oblong, brown
ARMS: short; beige cotton pads; claws
FEET: small; beige cotton pads; claws
STUFFING: excelsior and kapok mixture

Trademark

❧ Bingie ❧

1930s MERRYTHOUGHT LTD.

Bingie was part of a family of novelty teddies produced by Merrythought throughout the 1930s. He represents a sitting bear cub, and with his extremely soft filling and short, unjointed legs, he was intended to appeal to very young children. He was manufactured in seven sizes, with two extra-small sizes for babies, known as Baby Bingie.

EARS
The back of each ear is made from the same mohair plush as the body, while the inner part is white, now discolored, artifical silk plush.

EYES
Bingie has large amber glass eyes, positioned on either side of the central seam, low down on his face.

Short, stocky, swivel-jointed arms

STUFFING
He is particularly cuddly as he is stuffed with kapok. Fine excelsior is used as reinforcement behind the pads.

LEGS
His short, stocky legs are unjointed. They are sewn onto his body at a 90° angle so he is permanently in a sitting position.

Pads wider at heels and toes

Bear profile The large head, rounded back, and huge feet are all characteristics modeled on a real-life bear cub.

Clipped mohair muzzle

NOSE AND MOUTH
Vertical stitches of brown thread make up the large rectangular nose. Some long stitches reach from the tip of his muzzle down to his wide, stitched mouth.

Claws extend across plush and felt pads

CLAWS
Double stitching, in brown thread matching the nose and mouth, represents claws on the feet and paws.

Shaggy cream mohair, tipped brown

• BEAR ESSENTIALS •

HT: 14in (35cm)

FUR: brown-tipped cream, shaggy, mohair
EYES: large, amber, glass, black pupils
EARS: large, flat, placed high on head
MUZZLE: long, separate piece, clipped

NOSE: hand-embroidered, rectangular, brown
ARMS: short, stocky; rust felt pads; claws
FEET: large, long; rust felt pads; claws
STUFFING: kapok; fine excelsior in feet

MADE IN ENGLAND BY MERRYTHOUGHT LTD

Trademark

WINNIE-THE-POOH

W innie-the-Pooh is probably the best-known fictional bear in the world. Millions of copies of the book bearing his name as the title have been sold since it was first published by Methuen on October 14, 1926. It was subsequently translated into 22 languages, including Latin and Esperanto. Walt Disney made three cartoon films featuring the bear and his friends. Pooh stories have even been used to explain the principles of Taoism and, rather surprisingly, there is a street in Poland named after him.

THE EARLY YEARS

Winnie-the-Pooh started life as a real teddy bear, bought at the famous London store Harrods in 1921 by Dorothy Milne, wife of the author Alan Alexander Milne, for their son Christopher Robin's first birthday. The bear probably came from the factory of J.K. Farnell, since it made bears exclusively for Harrods at the time. Winnie-the-Pooh's original name was Edward Bear. He first appeared in 1924, in A.A. Milne's anthology of poetry for children, *When We Were Very Young*. His name was later changed to Winnie-the-Pooh. The name Winnie came from an American black bear in London Zoo, the mascot of a Canadian regiment from Winnipeg; Pooh was the name of Christopher Robin's favorite swan. In 1925, the Milnes moved from their London home to Cotchford Farm in Sussex, close to Ashdown Forest. The area became the setting of many of the stories, and is visited today by devotees.

◁ **Happy Family**
A.A. Milne, his six-year-old son Christopher Robin, and Winnie-the-Pooh, photographed in 1926.

△ **A Bear and His Honey**
This 1926 Shepard illustration shows Pooh protecting his honey from a flood.

△ **Final Home**
The original Winnie-the-Pooh is now in the New York Public Library.

△ Head in the Clouds
*Pooh pretends to be a cloud
so he can steal a pot of honey.*

POOH BEAR MEMORABILIA

A wealth of material still exists for Pooh admirers to enjoy. In Britain, the original pencil drawings can be viewed on request in London's Victoria and Albert Museum in South Kensington. They were donated by the artist Ernest Howard Shepard (1879-1976) when he was 90 years old. Shepard, who also illustrated Kenneth Grahame's *Wind in the Willows*, based his illustrations of Pooh Bear on his son's Steiff bear, "Growler," who unfortunately ended his days being mauled by a dog in Canada. In the Donnell branch of the New York Public Library, the original Pooh Bear, along with his friends Piglet, Tigger, and Kanga, is on display (Roo was lost in his owner's garden). In Britain, the stories were also well known through BBC Radio's *Children's Hour*, and The Teddy Toy Co. made toys and a board game with painted lead figures of the characters. The British company Chad Valley manufactured jigsaws, as well as heffalumps and a Christopher Robin doll. In the United States, collectors can keep an eye out for toys made by the New York-based F.W. Woolnough, or board games manufactured by Parker Brothers. In the 1940s and 1950s, Agnes Brush of Long Island was making Pooh bears.

WALT DISNEY'S POOH BEAR

Winnie-the-Pooh's popularity was renewed with the launching of a twenty-minute musical cartoon, *Winnie the Pooh and the Honey Tree*, by Walt Disney Studios in 1966. This was soon followed by *Winnie the Pooh and the Blustery Day*, and *Winnie the Pooh and Tigger Too*. In 1975, the three cartoons were combined to make a full-length feature film that proved then, as it is still today, very popular. Walt Disney's films meant that children growing up in this period knew a different Pooh from their parents and grandparents. This was a Pooh Bear that talked with an American accent, provided by the actor Sterling Holloway. He was plumper than the original Pooh and he wore a red shirt. Disney bought the rights to the character and licensed various companies to reproduce Winnie-the-Pooh as a stuffed toy. In 1988, the first annual Walt Disney World Teddy Bear Convention was held in Florida.

△ His Real Home
*Pooh's house was in fact a hollow
walnut tree in A.A. Milne's garden.
This was a favorite place for
Christopher Robin and his bear.*

▽ New Lease on Life for Drawings
*Pooh is rescued by Christopher Robin and friends
from Rabbit's burrow after eating too much honey
and condensed milk. Although he was well into his
nineties in 1973-1974, Methuen commissioned the
artist, E.H. Shepard, to give a new color wash to his
original illustrations.*

"Alex"

c. 1930 CHAD VALLEY

"Alex" has a button in his right ear. The Chad Valley button, which is celluloid over a metal base, is like the one used by Merrythought, one of Chad Valley's main British rivals. One of the first directors of Merrythought originally worked for Chad Valley – so perhaps he took the idea to Merrythought.

EARS
Like "Mr. Fluffy" *(see p.43)*, "Alex" has large flat ears. They are set close together along the top and upper sides of his head.

Protruding but blunt muzzle covered with clipped mohair

EYES
Amber glass eyes on wire shanks make this bear typical of his period. A touch of glue has also been added for extra strength, a common practice at this time.

ARMS
His long, curved, tapering arms end in large pads of brown brushed cotton.

Large feet with pads of brown brushed cotton, reinforced with cardboard

Long, mohair plush fur

Bear profile *Although reminiscent of the more traditional German bear, "Alex" is much plumper, a common feature of British bears belonging to this period.*

The black thread used for the nose has faded to brown

NOSE
Vertical stitches, with a horizontal stitch across the top, make up the nose.

STUFFING
The limbs are all kapok; the body and head are filled with a mixture of kapok and excelsior.

• BEAR ESSENTIALS •

HT: 17in (42cm)

FUR: golden, long, curly, mohair plush
EYES: medium, amber, glass, black pupils
EARS: large, flat, close together, top of head
MUZZLE: blunt, protruding, clipped mohair

NOSE: hand-embroidered, triangular, black
ARMS: long; brown brushed cotton pads; claws
FEET: large; brown brushed cotton pads; claws
STUFFING: kapok and excelsior mix, kapok

Printed lettering

Trademark

❧ "Heinrich" ❧

c. 1935 SCHREYER & CO.

"Heinrich" is an example of a Schuco Yes/No bear. He has a moving head operated from his tail. Adolf Kahn, the Jewish partner of the Schuco firm, escaped to England from Germany in 1934 and may well have passed the idea on to H.G. Stone for its Chiltern Wagmee series of 1937.

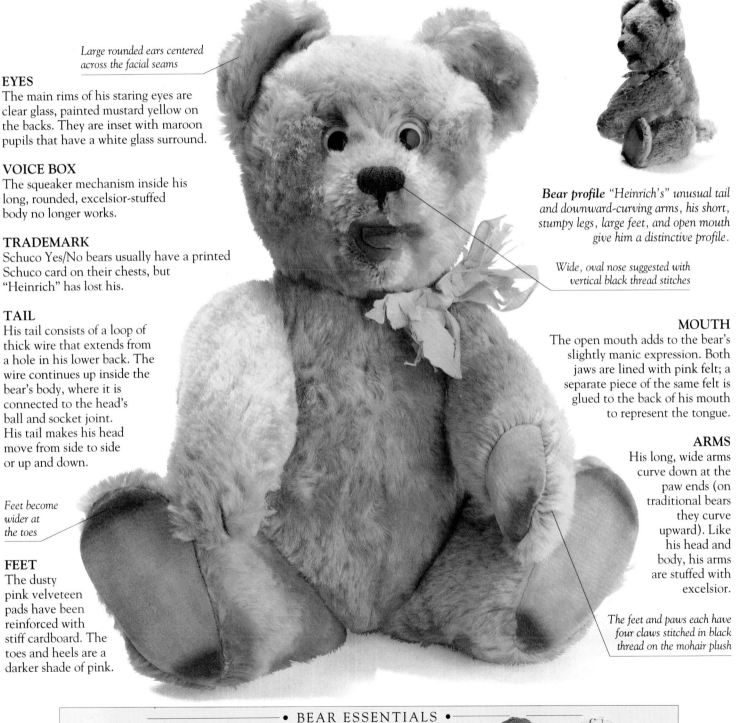

Large rounded ears centered across the facial seams

EYES
The main rims of his staring eyes are clear glass, painted mustard yellow on the backs. They are inset with maroon pupils that have a white glass surround.

VOICE BOX
The squeaker mechanism inside his long, rounded, excelsior-stuffed body no longer works.

TRADEMARK
Schuco Yes/No bears usually have a printed Schuco card on their chests, but "Heinrich" has lost his.

TAIL
His tail consists of a loop of thick wire that extends from a hole in his lower back. The wire continues up inside the bear's body, where it is connected to the head's ball and socket joint. His tail makes his head move from side to side or up and down.

Feet become wider at the toes

FEET
The dusty pink velveteen pads have been reinforced with stiff cardboard. The toes and heels are a darker shade of pink.

Bear profile *"Heinrich's" unusual tail and downward-curving arms, his short, stumpy legs, large feet, and open mouth give him a distinctive profile.*

Wide, oval nose suggested with vertical black thread stitches

MOUTH
The open mouth adds to the bear's slightly manic expression. Both jaws are lined with pink felt; a separate piece of the same felt is glued to the back of his mouth to represent the tongue.

ARMS
His long, wide arms curve down at the paw ends (on traditional bears they curve upward). Like his head and body, his arms are stuffed with excelsior.

The feet and paws each have four claws stitched in black thread on the mohair plush

---

• BEAR ESSENTIALS •

HT: 14in (36cm)

FUR: honey-colored, mohair plush
EYES: clear glass, yellow backs, maroon pupils
EARS: large, rounded, centered in face seams
MUZZLE: blunt, protruding; open mouth

NOSE: hand-embroidered, wide, oval, black
ARMS: large; pink velveteen pads; claws
FEET: wide; pink velveteen pads; claws
STUFFING: excelsior throughout bear

Trademark

❧ "Miss Jessie Criddle" ❧

1930s WOOLWORTH'S

"Miss Jessie Criddle" was originally bought in a Woolworth's in England before World War II. F.W. Woolworth is an American chain that opened its first store in Britain in 1909; by the early 1930s there were branches in most major towns. Made from low-quality plush, she is typical of inexpensive British bears of the time.

EARS
"Miss Jessie Criddle's" flat ears are large and floppy because they are made from thin plush. They sit toward the back of her head.

HEAD
The large domed head has a rounded, jutting-out chin that makes her muzzle quite unique.

Patch under right armpit

EYES
Her amber glass eyes are on wire hooks. Placed wide apart, they are sewn into the facial seam. Similar bears dating from the 1950s had plastic eyes on wire shanks.

STUFFING
The rather dark shade of excelsior, seen poking though holes in the paw pads, indicates that "Miss Jessie Criddle" is a low-quality bear.

FUR
"Miss Jessie Criddle" shows signs of wear and tear, and love and affection: her artificial silk plush fur is well worn for her age.

Thin curved paws

FEET
This bear's feet are large, rounded, and stocky. They are similar in shape to "Colin's" (see p.54).

***Bear profile** From this angle, you can see the bear's unusual protruding chin and short arms and feet. "Miss Jessie Criddle's" narrow hips are typical of a 1930s British bear.*

NOSE
Her nose is embroidered with black wool in vertical stitches. Two of the center stitches extend down to her mouth.

ARMS
The short, tapering arms are particularly wide near the shoulder. Her paws are covered in dark brown oilcloth.

Short artificial silk plush

CLAWS
Note that neither her feet nor her paws have embroidered claws, a feature that distinguishes her from earlier bears.

Well-worn oilcloth pads

• BEAR ESSENTIALS •

HT: 29in (73cm)

FUR: golden, short, artificial silk plush
EYES: medium, amber, glass, black pupils
EARS: large, flat, floppy, toward back of head
MUZZLE: square, protruding, jutting chin

NOSE: hand-embroidered, square, black
ARMS: short; brown oilcloth pads; no claws
FEET: stocky; brown oilcloth pads; no claws
STUFFING: excelsior throughout bear

DISTINGUISHING FEATURES: "Miss Jessie Criddle" has particularly large and floppy ears, owing to the thinness of the plush. The ears sit at the back of the head.

❧ "Mr. Jollyboy" ❧

LATE 1930s BRITISH

"Mr. Jollyboy" is very similar to "Miss Jessie Criddle" (see p.60) and may have been made in the same factory. He is a fine example of the many bears made of colored artificial silk plush that were produced in contrast to the more common shades of brown. These colored bears were made well into the 1950s and are sometimes difficult to date.

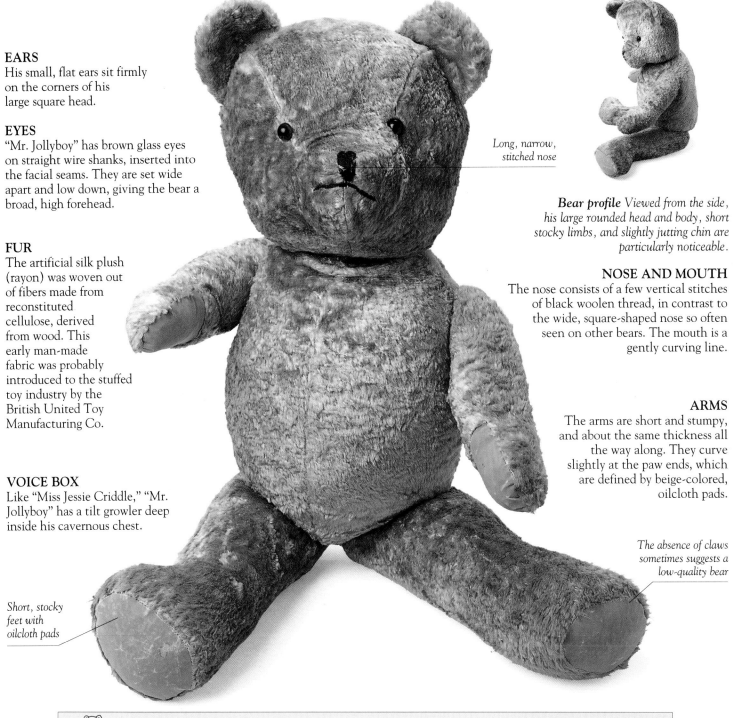

EARS
His small, flat ears sit firmly on the corners of his large square head.

EYES
"Mr. Jollyboy" has brown glass eyes on straight wire shanks, inserted into the facial seams. They are set wide apart and low down, giving the bear a broad, high forehead.

FUR
The artificial silk plush (rayon) was woven out of fibers made from reconstituted cellulose, derived from wood. This early man-made fabric was probably introduced to the stuffed toy industry by the British United Toy Manufacturing Co.

VOICE BOX
Like "Miss Jessie Criddle," "Mr. Jollyboy" has a tilt growler deep inside his cavernous chest.

Short, stocky feet with oilcloth pads

Long, narrow, stitched nose

Bear profile *Viewed from the side, his large rounded head and body, short stocky limbs, and slightly jutting chin are particularly noticeable.*

NOSE AND MOUTH
The nose consists of a few vertical stitches of black woolen thread, in contrast to the wide, square-shaped nose so often seen on other bears. The mouth is a gently curving line.

ARMS
The arms are short and stumpy, and about the same thickness all the way along. They curve slightly at the paw ends, which are defined by beige-colored, oilcloth pads.

The absence of claws sometimes suggests a low-quality bear

• BEAR ESSENTIALS •

HT: 28in (70cm)

FUR: pale blue, woven artificial silk plush
EYES: small, brown, glass, placed wide apart
EARS: small, flat, in corners of square head
MUZZLE: square, large, with protruding chin

NOSE: hand-embroidered, long, thin, black
ARMS: short; beige oilcloth pads; no claws
FEET: short; beige oilcloth pads; no claws
STUFFING: excelsior throughout bear

DISTINGUISHING FEATURES: The artificial silk plush, along with the unusual vertical nose and jutting-out chin, differentiate this bear from his contemporaries.

❧ "Arthur van Gelden" ❧

1930s DUTCH

"Arthur van Gelden's" present owner bought him from a Dutch dealer. Because he is similar to other bears of Dutch origin, it is assumed that he was made in Holland. In appearance, he could be confused with low-price English bears of the same period, but his tremendous weight distinguishes him from them.

EARS
His large ears occupy the corners of his head. They are slightly curved to give a cupped effect.

EYES
The googly, or cartoon-style, black and white eyes are made from slightly convex, enameled metal buttons. The ring at the back, similar to the type used behind shoe button eyes, is sewn onto the mohair plush.

CLAWS
In keeping with other large, inexpensive bears ("Miss Jessie Criddle" and "Mr. Jollyboy," for example), "Arthur van Gelden" has no embroidered claws.

FUR
"Arthur van Gelden" is made with short-pile artifical silk plush. A golden color is used for most of his body, but the foot pads and paws are both white.

Bear profile "Arthur van Gelden" has a long, domed head. His body is straight and rectangular with short, stumpy legs. Note how there is only a slight indentation for the neck.

The nose and mouth are stitched with black thread

NOSE
The long, narrow nose is defined with a series of vertical stitches, similar to "Miss Jessie Criddle's" nose (*see p.60*).

The arms are short, straight, and slightly tapered

STUFFING
This bear is stuffed very tightly with excelsior, giving him a heavy, solid appearance. It is unlikely that he had a voice box – the solid stuffing would have made any noise inaudible.

Large rounded feet

• BEAR ESSENTIALS •

HT: 28in (70cm)

FUR: golden, short, artificial silk plush
EYES: medium, enameled, metal buttons
EARS: large, rounded, slightly cupped
MUZZLE: blunt, protruding, upward curve

NOSE: hand-embroidered, narrow, black
ARMS: straight; white plush pads; no claws
FEET: large; white plush pads; no claws
STUFFING: very compact excelsior

DISTINGUISHING FEATURES: "Arthur van Gelden" is a solid, heavy teddy bear. His enameled button eyes, narrow nose, and white pads all help with identification.

"Marcel"

1920s FRENCH

The majority of teddy bears for sale in France were imported from Germany, until the limited supply caused by World War I stimulated the establishment of French factories. Rivaling Steiff, metal button trademarks were sometimes used in the ear or, as in the case of "Marcel," on the body, for identification.

EYES
The small glass eyes have the remains of paint on their backs. They are held on wire shanks sewn into the bear's face.

Small rounded ears are set across his facial seams toward the back of his head

VOICE BOX
An oval squeaker mechanism in "Marcel's" long, thin body still works.

FEET
His relatively large feet have thin ankles in the Steiff tradition. The brown felt used for the pads is a different shade from that used on the paws, although it is difficult to tell which are replacements.

TRADEMARK
A gold metal button clipped to the bear's chest is an idea borrowed from Steiff. The French may also have copied the concept of a raised symbol from the German company. Illustrations of hugging bears on buttons appeared in Steiff catalogs dating from before World War I.

The ankles are very thin

Short, cinnamon-colored mohair plush

Bear profile *From this angle you can see "Marcel's" long, thin body, large feet, narrow paws, and pointed muzzle, with an unusual squashed nose.*

NOSE AND MOUTH
The black stitching for the nose and mouth is at a slight angle and not very neat, indicating, perhaps, that it was the work of an untrained seamstress.

ARMS
The long, thin, tapering arms end in small, narrow paws with dark brown felt pads.

CLAWS
There are three claws on each foot and each paw. They are stitched in black thread.

The claws are stitched across the mohair plush and brown felt

---

• BEAR ESSENTIALS •

HT: 15in (38cm)

FUR: cinnamon-colored, short, mohair plush
EYES: small, glass, black-painted backs
EARS: small, curved, toward back of head
MUZZLE: thin, protruding, and pointed

NOSE: hand-embroidered, rectangular, black
ARMS: small; dark brown felt pads; claws
FEET: large; brown felt pads; claws
STUFFING: excelsior throughout bear

Raised lettering and logo

Trademark

"Didcock"

1938 J.K. FARNELL

"Didcock," with his Alpha toy trademark, would have been manufactured at Farnell's London factory. Built after World War I, the operation was destroyed by fire in 1934 and rebuilt the following year, only to be razed to the ground when the city was bombed in 1940. Alpha bears remained a popular line until 1968.

EARS
The ears are relatively large and slightly cupped.

Ears are partly concealed by the shaggy fur

EYES
"Didcock" has unusual black button eyes. Said by his owner to be original, they add greatly to his charm and appeal.

ARMS
He has long, tapering arms based on the traditional teddy bear style. They are distinctly curved at the paw ends, making them lie gracefully in his lap.

STUFFING
His head and arms are stuffed with excelsior, and his legs are filled with kapok. His body is filled with a mixture of both materials.

The feet are large compared with the short legs

Bear profile *The side view demonstrates that Farnell followed the traditional teddy bear shape based on Steiff, rather than the one introduced by rivals in Britain.*

NOSE
His square nose consists of vertical stitches of black thread. His crooked mouth makes him look bemused.

Claws are embroidered on each paw and foot with black thread

TRADEMARK
The woven label has the Alpha trademark, registered in 1925.

• BEAR ESSENTIALS •

HT: 15in (38cm)

FUR: long, blond, curly mohair plush
EYES: small, black, plastic buttons
EARS: large, slightly cupped and concealed
MUZZLE: protruding from flat forehead

NOSE: hand-embroidered, square, black
ARMS: curved; beige cotton pads; claws
FEET: large; beige cotton pads; claws
STUFFING: excelsior, kapok and mix

Trademark

❧ "Senior Mr. Roosevelt" ❧

c. 1940 KNICKERBOCKER TOY CO. INC.

This American company had been making stuffed toys and bears since the early 1900s. Originally based in New York (where this bear was made), the firm later moved to New Jersey and imported sewn component parts from Korea. Although the firm no longer exists, it is noted for its Smokey Bears, made in the 1960s and 1970s.

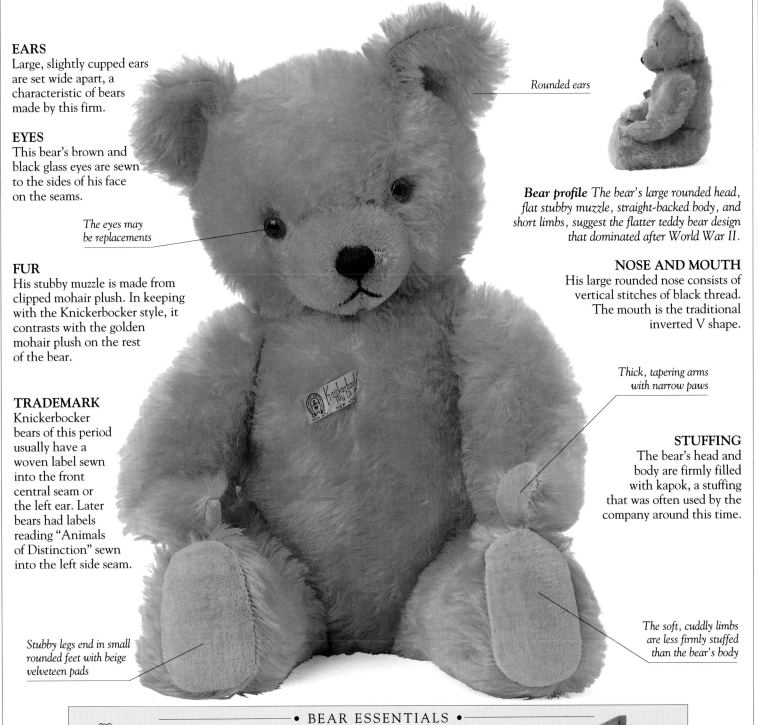

EARS
Large, slightly cupped ears are set wide apart, a characteristic of bears made by this firm.

EYES
This bear's brown and black glass eyes are sewn to the sides of his face on the seams.

The eyes may be replacements

FUR
His stubby muzzle is made from clipped mohair plush. In keeping with the Knickerbocker style, it contrasts with the golden mohair plush on the rest of the bear.

TRADEMARK
Knickerbocker bears of this period usually have a woven label sewn into the front central seam or the left ear. Later bears had labels reading "Animals of Distinction" sewn into the left side seam.

Stubby legs end in small rounded feet with beige velveteen pads

Rounded ears

***Bear profile** The bear's large rounded head, flat stubby muzzle, straight-backed body, and short limbs, suggest the flatter teddy bear design that dominated after World War II.*

NOSE AND MOUTH
His large rounded nose consists of vertical stitches of black thread. The mouth is the traditional inverted V shape.

Thick, tapering arms with narrow paws

STUFFING
The bear's head and body are firmly filled with kapok, a stuffing that was often used by the company around this time.

The soft, cuddly limbs are less firmly stuffed than the bear's body

---

• BEAR ESSENTIALS •

HT: 20in (51cm)

FUR: golden mohair plush, clipped mohair	NOSE: hand-embroidered, oval, black
EYES: small, brown and black, glass, wide-set	ARMS: short; beige velveteen pads; no claws
EARS: large, rounded, cupped, set wide apart	FEET: small; beige velveteen pads; no claws
MUZZLE: short, rounded, blunt, clipped	STUFFING: kapok throughout bear

Trademark

❧ "Edward" ❧

1940s AUSTRALIAN OR BRITISH

Now living in a vicarage in the south of England, "Edward" was his owner's friend and companion during her childhood in Australia. He is made of sheepskin dyed golden brown, and he is a typical example of a teddy bear produced during World War II, when traditional mohair plush was in short supply.

EARS
These are made of two narrow semicircles of sheepskin, sewn into the corners of his square head.

Golden-brown sheepskin

EYES
His eyes are made of clear glass. Tiny amounts of paint suggest they were once painted brown on the backs. The pupils are black. The wire shanks are sewn onto his face with thick thread knotted at the back of his head.

VOICE BOX
This bear's tilt growler is made of an early mottled green plastic. The base is marked "Kim Toys Made in England." It is possible that the voice box was exported to be used in an Australian-made bear. Alternatively, the whole toy may have been exported from England.

FEET
His feet show little ankle definition. The leather pads are oversewn with large stitches of black cotton – some may be repair work. He has no claws.

Short, oval, black leather pads

Unjointed head

Bear profile *Manufacturers tried to retain the traditional teddy bear design, but wartime shortages forced them to use thicker, less flexible materials. As a result of this, his back has no hump and his head is relatively flat.*

NOSE
The round, gray leather nose is probably a replacement. The original would have matched the bear's black leather pads. The new nose is larger than the original, perhaps covering worn sheepskin on the muzzle and mouth.

The tapered, curved arms are in the style of contemporary British bears

JOINTS
"Edward" has small cardboard disk joints in both his legs and arms. The bear has no head joint.

STUFFING
The head and limbs are filled with excelsior, the body with an excelsior and cotton waste wadding mix.

• BEAR ESSENTIALS •

HT: 21in (53cm)

FUR: golden-brown, dyed sheepskin
EYES: medium, clear glass, black pupils
EARS: narrow, semicircles of sheepskin
MUZZLE: blunt, wide, slightly protruding

NOSE: leather patch, large, round, gray
ARMS: short; black leather pads; no claws
FEET: small; black leather pads; no claws
STUFFING: excelsior, excelsior/cotton

DISTINGUISHING FEATURES: Wartime shortages forced the manufacturers to use sheepskin for fur instead of the traditional woven mohair plush.

❧ "Chili Pepper" ❧

1940s H.G. STONE & CO. LTD.

"Chili" is an example of a Chiltern stuffed toy, so called because the British firm's factory was in the Chiltern Hills of Buckinghamshire. He is a musical teddy bear belonging to the Hugmee line. He plays "Brahms' Lullaby" when wound up; earlier Chiltern teddies played tunes when their bodies were pressed.

EARS
His almost circular ears are positioned toward the back of his head. Set wide apart, the inner edges are turned slightly and caught in the seams of his face.

EYES
The amber glass eyes with black pupils are attached to short wire hooks. The hooks are sewn onto his face with strong white thread that goes through his head and is fastened in the back, near his neck.

VOICE BOX
The clockwork musical mechanism works on the Swiss comb and toothed-cylinder principle *(see p.37)*. Housed in a square metal canister covered in white gauze, it is fitted into the lower back of his body. The key sticks out through a brasslike metal grommet on his back.

His coloring is an unusual coral pink

FUR
Unlike most bears in the Hugmee line, who were covered with mohair plush, "Chili" is made from artificial silk plush. This man-made fabric was popular with certain other stuffed toy manufacturers at the time.

Bear profile This view shows the dents that mark where his eyes are tied off at the back of his head and the key for his internal music box. Notice how his large round muzzle occupies most of his face.

NOSE AND MOUTH
Hand-embroidered in black thread, his nose is rectangular. The small inverted V of his mouth creates the characteristic glum expression of a Chiltern Hugmee bear.

Relatively short arms

CLAWS
Four short claws of black thread are stitched to each paw. On the foot pads there are four claws, suggested with diagonal stitches reaching across the pad onto the artificial silk plush.

STUFFING
Cotton wadding makes "Chili" cuddly.

Beige velveteen pads on small feet

• BEAR ESSENTIALS •

HT: 16in (42cm)

FUR: coral pink, woven artificial silk plush
EYES: small, amber, glass with black pupils
EARS: rounded, wide apart, turned slightly
MUZZLE: large, rounded, short but wide

NOSE: hand-embroidered, rectangular, black
ARMS: short; beige velveteen pads; claws
FEET: small; beige velveteen pads; claws
STUFFING: pale blue cotton waste wadding

TRADEMARK: "Chili Pepper" may once have had a small fabric label bearing the company's trade name, Chiltern Toys. He may also have had a cardboard swing tag.

SMOKEY THE BEAR

Smokey the Bear is the popular symbol of the U.S. Forest Fire Prevention Campaign. He first appeared on a poster in 1944 with the message, "Smokey says: Care will prevent nine out of ten fires." He immediately won the hearts of the American people. His popularity was boosted by the arrival at the National Zoo in Washington, D.C. in 1950, of a bear cub that had been wounded in a fire in New Mexico's Lincoln National Forest. The cub was named Smokey, and for the rest of his life in the zoo, he was visited by thousands of children.

CAMPAIGN AGAINST FOREST FIRES

In the 1940s, a spate of fires devastated large areas of forest in the United States, making it essential to find a powerful new character to promote the Forest Fire Prevention Campaign. A bear seemed the obvious choice; the forest is their natural habitat, and bears are known for their strength. The name Smokey was borrowed from Smokey Joe Martin, who worked for the New York City Fire Department during the 1920s. Albert Staehle, an artist with *The Saturday Evening Post*, was the original illustrator of Smokey, who became known as the "guardian of the forest." Staehle portrayed the bear, putting out a camp fire with a bucket of water, on a poster produced by the Wartime Advertising Council. The earliest illustrations of Smokey the Bear show him undressed, although it was not long before he was given his now-familiar denim jeans and ranger hat. As the years went on, he became less bearlike.

▽ **Ideal Bear**
The first Smokey the Bear was made by Ideal in 1953. He had a vinyl head, feet, and hands.

SMOKEY BEAR ACT

So great was his popularity that in May 1952 the "Smokey Bear Act" was passed by Congress to protect the exploitation of the character. Only the United States Department of State Foresters and the Advertising Council could authorize the manufacture of Smokey products, with fees going toward the prevention of forest fires.

▷ **Smokey Artifacts**
A pair of child's binoculars – for spotting both wildlife and forest fires – has a leather case decorated with Smokey's face. Items like these are very popular with collectors today.

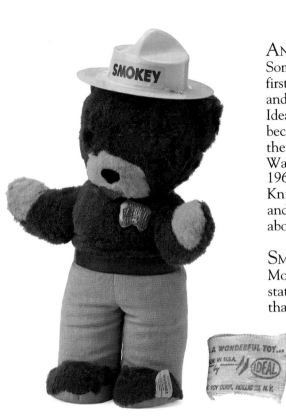

An Important Bear
Some of the early licensed Smokey items, such as the Ideal Company's first Smokey stuffed toy (1953), and the second version with a vinyl face and all-in-one jeans, which followed a year later, are highly collectible. Ideal also invented an application form for proud Smokey owners to become Junior Forest Rangers, a popular novelty. This resulted in the bear having his own address: Smokey the Bear Headquarters, Washington, D.C. 20252. A third Ideal Smokey was introduced in the 1960s. Several other American firms, such as Dakin and the Knickerbocker Toy Co., produced their own versions during the 1960s and 1970s, including Smokey Bears that could talk and give advice about preventing forest fires.

Smokey Collectibles
Molded figurines, mugs, money boxes, ashtrays, clocks, clothing, and stationery are among the large quantity of Smokey the Bear memorabilia that has been produced over the years. Many educational posters featuring the bear were sold including an early talking cardboard poster, printed with his face. On the back there was a pull-string voice box. Books and songs have been written about him, and he continues to be a figure of great importance and popular appeal in the prevention of forest fires.

△ *1960s Version*
Ideal's third version of Smokey was created in the 1960s. He was made from plush with all-in-one jeans. Like earlier versions, he is instantly recognizable because he wears a Smokey Ranger badge, belt, and hat.

▽ *Ranger Hats*
A Smokey Ranger hat, sold in child and adult sizes.

◁ *Take Care*
A Smokey the Bear figurine wearing denim jeans and carrying the familiar shovel. He has his hand raised in the "Take Care" pose.

▷ *Contemporary Smokey*
This modern Smokey the Bear stuffed toy was manufactured by Three Bears Inc. of Newport, Rhode Island, in 1985.

THE SYNTHETIC TEDDY BEAR

Although the years immediately after World War II saw a decrease in teddy bear production, the 1950s and 1960s witnessed the re-emergence of the teddy bear phenomenon. Bears made during this period were radically different from prewar designs. The ever-increasing availability of new materials, stemming from prewar developments in the field of plastics, revolutionized the industry. Various cartoon characters created by American animators also stimulated some manufacturers to create bears that were caricatures, such as Merrythought's Cheeky (see p.83), as well as sophisticated gimmickry, like Dean's 1967 perfumed bear, Scenty Bear, and Chad Valley's 1968 pull-string talking bear.

A NEW GENERATION

By 1960, many teddy bear manufacturers were using woven, and later knitted, nylon plush fabric. In Britain, for example, Dean's Childsplay, a subsidiary of Dean's Rag Book Co. offered a De-Luxe Bri-Nylon teddy bear in 1965. (Bri-Nylon was the registered trademark of ICI, who produced several synthetic fabrics.) Another fabric, Acrilan, woven from an acrylic fiber, was produced by Monsanto in the United States. During this period, experiments were also underway to develop a safe plastic eye to replace the early eyes attached precariously to easily broken wire shanks. Wendy Boston Playsafe Toys patented a rust-proof screw-locked eye in the late 1940s, which was later perfected using molded nylon for both screw and nut.

∇ **Machine-washable Bear**
Wendy Boston nylon plush bears.

THE MACHINE-WASHABLE BEAR

The use of artificial fabrics and plastic eyes made it possible for Wendy Boston to create the first completely machine-washable bear. Before this, bears could not be immersed in water: sodden excelsior was difficult to dry, damp kapok stained fabrics, even rayon did not take kindly to water. Nylon, in contrast, did, and combined with a water-repellent and quick-drying filling, such as polyurethane or latex foams in granular form, unbreakable eyes, and the omission of cardboard joints, the machine-washable bear was born. Wendy

△ **Royal Bear**
This was manufactured by Merrythought in honor of Queen Elizabeth II's coronation in 1953.

△ **TV Appearance**
The complete washability of the Wendy Boston bear was demonstrated on television in 1955.

◁ **Fashion Bears**
Mary Quant, 1960s trendsetter, with her own teddy bears.

Boston advertised the amazing breakthrough for the first time on television in 1955. This led to a phenomenon unique to a postwar generation – the teddy bear pegged to a wash line by his ears. The latter part of this teddy era saw the rise of American stuffed toy firms, such as Dakin and Wallace Berrie, which contracted out much of their work to Far Eastern countries, including Taiwan, Korea, and China, where labor was cheaper. Several famous names associated with the British teddy bear could not compete; by the late 1960s companies such as J.K. Farnell, Wendy Boston, and H.G. Stone had either folded or had been bought by larger companies. The increase in competition was also marked by the introduction of new equipment into toy factories so production could be stepped up. Wind-filling machines, for example, brought stuffing by hand to an end. In the new system, compressed air propelled the filling material through a narrow pipe, over which the opening of the teddy bear's limb, head, or body would be fitted. Some of these machines could fill toys 500 times faster than previously. Mechanical cutters that could stamp out several pieces of plush fabric at a time replaced the old method of cutting out individual templates, and also helped improve factory efficiency.

Δ **Bri-Nylon**
This tradename was registered in 1960.

Δ **The Ever-popular Teddy**
After the war, the new-look teddy proved just as popular as the earlier designs.

∇ **X-rayed Bear**
An X-ray of an American tumbling bear, revealing that both plastic and metal have been used in the bear's internal structure.

NEW SAFETY STANDARDS

During this period, governments turned their attention to regulations regarding toy safety. The British Standards Institution, for example, issued several Codes of Safety between 1958 and 1968, offering recommendations and test requirements. As a result, teddy bears became the subject of arson attacks by white-coated scientists experimenting with different yarns to produce inherently nonflammable fabrics or searching for flame-resistant solutions for their treatment. Heavy weights of 30 pounds, or more, were secured to teddy bears' eyes to see whether they would withstand abuse by human fingernails or teeth. Hygiene was also an issue, and new regulations demanded the testing of stuffings to determine cleanliness. As a result, many English teddy bears boasted possession of a Certificate of Hygiene.

a PLAY SAFE toy
made in
GT. BRITAIN
by
WENDY BOSTON

Δ **Innovator's Stamp**
Wendy Boston's trademark dates from 1959.

∇ **Tumbling Bear**
Wind up this bear's arm and see him tumble.

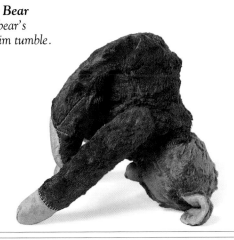

BEAR NECESSITIES

*R*ationing continued to create shortages immediately *after World War II, but soon teddy bear manufacturing was revolutionized by the use of synthetic materials. With the help of new technology, as well as a greater awareness of safety standards, stuffed toy producers began to create the first completely man-made, fully washable, almost indestructible teddy bear.*

Glass eye

Plastic eyes

NOSE
Black molded rubber noses were first introduced on some bears in the 1950s.

Wendy Boston eye

PLASTIC EYES
By the 1950s, plastic eyes were common. Wendy Boston patented its screw-in, molded nylon eye in 1948. Similar plastic eyes followed. The safe lock-in eyes had washers; some of the earlier plastic eyes had wire shanks; later ones had plastic shanks with washers.

Plastic safe eye

Leg joint disk
Arm joint disk

Hardboard disks with plastic pin

Hardboard disks with cotter pin

Cardboard disk with metal washer

JOINTS
Jointing systems continued to be made with cardboard or hardboard disks and metal washers, although manufacturers experimented with the use of plastic for both the disks and pins.

c. 1965 BRITISH
A bear made by Pedigree Soft Toys Ltd. with woven Bri-Nylon plush, plastic foam stuffing, and safe lock-in plastic eyes.

1960s synthetic plush

Golden mohair plush

1950s acrylic plush

BELL
In 1957, Merrythought made a bear with a bell in each ear; other firms copied the idea throughout the late 1950s and early 1960s.

Hollow globe of metal alloy holds small leadlike pellet

FUR
After World War II, many manufacturers turned to synthetic fabrics, such as acrylic and nylon plush, that could be made in various colors and piles. Natural mohair plush was still used, however.

THREAD
Synthetic-based threads, such as nylon and polyester, began to replace cotton for machine stitching.

Cotton thread

Synthetic-based thread

Sheepskin

Excelsior

DETAILS
Noses, mouths, and claws were mostly embroidered in the traditional way, with black or brown thread.

Synthetic plush

Ultrasuede

Cardboard

REINFORCED PADS
Many bears produced in the traditional style continued to have foot and paw pads reinforced with cardboard.

Embroidery thread

PAD FABRICS
Traditional-style bears continued to have pads made from felt, and Rexine faded out in the late 1950s. Woven cotton fabric and velveteen remained popular until the 1960s, when they were replaced by synthetic equivalents, such as Ultrasuede. Manufacturers of unjointed, washable teddy bears used the same synthetic plush for the pads as the rest of the body, but chose a differing color or pile (in the past a contrasting fabric was used).

Rexine

Woven cotton fabric

Velveteen

Felt

GROWLERS
Tilt growlers with sliding, weighted bellows remained popular during this period; the cardboard canisters often had perforated tin "speakers." Cardboard lids were still used, and all-plastic containers became available in the 1940s. Cardboard and oilcloth squeakers remained almost unchanged, except for the occasional use of the external reed encased in cardboard.

Tin speaker

Squeaker with external reed

Squeakers with internal reeds

STUFFING
Excelsior and kapok, and kapok substitute (sub) made from the waste of textile mills, were still used. By the 1950s, however, many manufacturers were turning to plastic foam, a completely synthetic, spongelike substance (usually shredded), that helped them to create the machine-washable teddy bear.

Kapok

Sub

Shredded plastic foam

MUSIC BOX
The traditional Swiss clock-work movement was still commonly used, although a molded nylon cover often replaced the all-metal casing.

Music box with plastic cover

BEAR APPAREL

In the years following World War II, teddy's wardrobe was less imaginative as manufacturers were restricted in the types of materials they could use. During this period, the teddy bear's shape changed. His head became enormous and his limbs short and stumpy, making him difficult to clothe stylishly. Fewer and fewer clothes were made professionally, and the teddy bear tended to depend on dolls' castoffs, or its young owner's first tentative knitting skills. Many teddy bears were made with soft, colorful, synthetic fabrics, and this, combined with an increasingly unbearlike shape, led to their role as a tactile comforter, rather than as a character with a costume. Today's collectors often make their teddies' clothes themselves.

ALL-IN-ONE BEAR

Many of the dressed bears prevalent in the years before World War II were still being made during the 1950s, which can sometimes make dating difficult for collectors. Teddy bears with all-in-one clothes and bodies were particularly common during this period of economic stringency. It enabled manufacturers to save on plush, although it meant that children would, and indeed did, miss out on the dressing and the undressing of their teddy bears. Although the teddy bear lacked exquisite dress sense in this period, many companies made some effort to dress their teddy bears in some style. The Paris company ALFA had been making all-in-one teddy bears since 1935, and in the 1950s it was offering particularly feminine bears. These bears would be dressed in blue or red gingham dresses, trimmed with lace and ribbon, and wearing matching slippers.

△ **Tartan Ted**
A sheepskin bear in tartan.

THE CHEEKY DYNASTY

Across the Channel, in England, Merrythought's Cheeky bear, first introduced in 1957 (see p.83), was produced with a woven fabric body and limbs that represented clothes. However, the trousers and suspenders, and dress and apron, worn by Mr. and Mrs. Twisty Cheeky of 1966-68 (with their unique internal wire frames that could bend in all directions) could be removed from their suede bodies.

◁ **Indian Attire**
"Kensington" dates from 1918, although he wears a stunning embroidered and bespangled child's jacket that was bought in the northern Indian state of Uttar, Pradesh, in the 1960s.

△ **Rupert Bear Look-alike**
With his knitted red sweater and yellow-checked trousers, he is dressed to resemble the cartoon character Rupert Bear.

A STEP BACK

Steiff reintroduced some teddy bears in the 1950s that had originally been produced before World War II. Teddyli, who had a head of either dark brown or blond plush and an open or closed mouth, was based directly on Teddy Baby of the 1930s *(see p.49)*. Teddyli's soft fabric body with dangling, unstuffed arms and straight, standing feet, however, make him unique to this period. He came dressed in a variety of delightful costumes, including Bavarian dirndl (full, gathered) skirts and Austrian lederhosen (leather shorts). Some Teddylis had rubber bodies – unfortunate for collectors, as rubber tends to crumble. The special edition Nimrod Teddy, produced in 1953 for the Steiff teddy bear's 50th birthday, is particularly sought after now. This nine-inch bear was dressed as a huntsman, and came in four different colors wearing a felt tunic and cap and carrying a wooden rifle. Small Zotty bears were also produced in the late 1960s, wearing felt rompers or jackets with caps.

TEDDY BEAR PERSONALITIES

By the 1950s, a host of new teddy bear personalities were becoming popular through books, newspapers, comics, and the new medium of television. It was not long before children chose to dress their own bear in the costume of their favorite character. Television provided plenty of ideas. In Britain, the popular children's program, *Blue Peter*, which had been running since 1958, demonstrated many inventive ideas on how to dress teddy bears. The accompanying book is still proving useful for many of today's teddy bear collectors.

△ **Flower Power**
Sophie is very much a product of the 1960s. Her shape does not take conventional clothes, so she has flowers and a jacket embroidered onto her body instead.

◁ **Tank Top Ted**
Many teddy bear owners dress their bears in the fashion of the time. This bear's tank top dates him to the late 1960s.

▷ **Traveling Ted**
This suitcase was probably made as a doll's accessory or as part of a novelty sewing kit. It is perfect for the teddy who likes to travel.

◁ **"Parlez-vous français?"**
A bear dressed as a Frenchman, with a blue beret, blue and white striped top, and blue dungarees. His brilliant red bow and Eiffel Tower brooch complete the outfit.

BEAR MEMORABILIA

The era following the difficult days of World War II brought with it various technological advances and the arrival of new synthetic materials. A shift in industrial world power toward the Far East – Japan, especially – and the accompanying baby boom period in the West resulted in numerous, cheaply made, colorful, and ingenious teddy bear-inspired novelties. At the same time, the teddy bear was given a new lease on life through the emergence of cartoon characters, such as Baloo Bear in Walt Disney's film version of Kipling's The Jungle Book, and through the popular English comic book, Teddy Bear.

△ 1950s Bear Doll
A hard plastic, jointed doll made by Rosebud Dolls.

SYNTHETIC BEARIANA

By the 1960s, celluloid – a flammable material that had been used to make dolls – had been banned as a dangerous substance, and toy manufacturers resorted to soft or hard vinyl, which was relatively cheap and easy to mold into teddy bears. British firms, including Rosebud and Rodnoid, made straightforward, jointed copies of the traditional bear. Other firms, including Dunbee and Casdon, made squeaker toys, push-alongs, money boxes, and toothbrush holders. Rubber versions of Punkinhead, the Cheekylike bear *(see p.83)* made by Merrythought for the Canadian market, were produced from 1948-1956. Japan also made mechanical bears in vast quantities from 1950-1970. The appeal of these popular bears lies in the often humorous domestic scenes that are portrayed, such as a mother feeding a baby, a visit to the dentist, or the boss at the office. Sometimes, these toys have ingenious mechanisms that allow up to seven actions to take place, including eyes lighting up and the expulsion of water.

◁ Bookworm Bear
A 1950s Japanese bear with a clockwork mechanism and a magnet that makes his arm flip through the pages.

▷ Russian Bear
This Russian clockwork bear repeatedly raises his arm to lick his ice cream, while at the same time, he turns around on the spot.

△ Glove Puppet
This teddy bear, called Sooty, is constructed around a glove. When the wearer wiggles his fingers, the bear takes on a life of his own.

TELEVISION TEDDIES

Starting in the early 1950s, new teddy bear characters were introduced through the medium of television, which had become a way of life in many homes. Perhaps the most famous animated bears brought into millions of homes worldwide in the 1960s were Yogi Bear (named after Yogi Berra, the baseball player) and his friends, Boo Boo and Cindy. They were the creation of the American cartoon makers Hanna-Barbera. Merchandising soon included a wide range of stuffed toys. Australia has its own ursine television personality, Humphrey B. Bear, who first appeared in a show for preschool children in the early 1960s. Classic Toys created its own Humphrey B. Bear, who wears a tartan vest and a boater – he is now particularly collectible. Other firms made related products, such as plastic versions of Humphrey B. Bear and printed cloth covered in images of him. Many are now popular with collectors.

△ The Three Bears
These three plastic bears with painted clothes date from the 1950s.

Sooty, created by an English electrical engineer and amateur magician, Harry Corbett, made his debut on British television with his squeaky dog friend, Sweep, in 1952. Several companies produced related items. Chad Valley was given sole rights to reproduce the glove puppet, now a collectors' item, especially if complete with a wooden wand. Since 1980, however, the puppets have been made in Taiwan and distributed by Patsy B. Marketing. Sooty fans have their own club and museum, based near Harry Corbett's home, and the show continues today in the hands of his son, Matthew.

▷ Rattle
A 1950s Japanese synthetic plush bear in the shape of a child's rattle. His bulbous pantaloons contain jingling bells.

△ Purse
A 1940s teddy bear that doubles as a money purse with an oilcloth lining. It looks worn out and was probably a favorite of its young owner. The purse could be a forerunner of the teddy bear backpack that became popular in the 1980s.

◁ Teddy's Playtime
This English bone china mug dates from the 1960s. It has a Royal Albert design called Teddy's Playtime. Ceramic ware was also decorated with teddy bear characters.

❧ *"Horst"* ❧

1953 GEBRUDER HERMANN

This little bear was made at the new Hermann factory in Hirschaid, in the American Zone of Germany (Bernhard Hermann had moved there in 1948). Hermann bears continued to rival those made in the Steiff factory: the one shown here is often confused with the Steiff Zotty, also introduced in the 1950s.

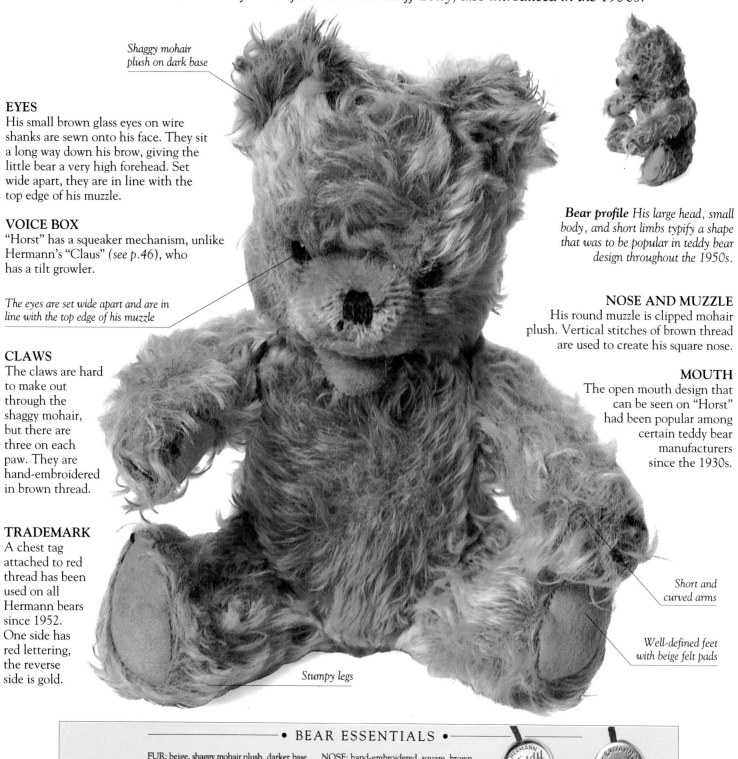

Shaggy mohair plush on dark base

EYES
His small brown glass eyes on wire shanks are sewn onto his face. They sit a long way down his brow, giving the little bear a very high forehead. Set wide apart, they are in line with the top edge of his muzzle.

VOICE BOX
"Horst" has a squeaker mechanism, unlike Hermann's "Claus" *(see p.46)*, who has a tilt growler.

The eyes are set wide apart and are in line with the top edge of his muzzle

CLAWS
The claws are hard to make out through the shaggy mohair, but there are three on each paw. They are hand-embroidered in brown thread.

TRADEMARK
A chest tag attached to red thread has been used on all Hermann bears since 1952. One side has red lettering, the reverse side is gold.

Bear profile *His large head, small body, and short limbs typify a shape that was to be popular in teddy bear design throughout the 1950s.*

NOSE AND MUZZLE
His round muzzle is clipped mohair plush. Vertical stitches of brown thread are used to create his square nose.

MOUTH
The open mouth design that can be seen on "Horst" had been popular among certain teddy bear manufacturers since the 1930s.

Short and curved arms

Well-defined feet with beige felt pads

Stumpy legs

❧ BEAR ESSENTIALS ❧

HT: 10in (25cm)

FUR: beige, shaggy mohair plush, darker base
EYES: small, brown, glass, black pupils
EARS: small, flat and standing upright
MUZZLE: clipped mohair plush, protruding

NOSE: hand-embroidered, square, brown
ARMS: short, curved; beige felt pads; claws
FEET: small; beige felt pads; claws
STUFFING: excelsior throughout bear

Trademark

❧ "Ross" ❧

c. 1950 BRITISH

"Ross" is typical of British bears made in the 1940s and early 1950s, but he has one distinctive feature: his mouth can be opened and closed using a lever at the back of his head. Other bears had mouths that worked when their owners pressed the stomach, tipped the head back, or pulled a ring located in the back of the bear's neck.

EARS
"Ross" has wide, flat ears centered over the seams of his face. Much of the mohair plush has worn away.

Short, blunt muzzle

MOUTH
Two pieces of hinged board in his mouth extend into the back of his head, where the ends are held apart by a large spring covered with gauze. Two metal rods connected to the board poke out from the back of the bear's head, where each is tipped with a round ball of amber glass.

Pink felt-lined mouth

STUFFING
"Ross" is stuffed with cotton waste wadding and some shredded stockinette. He has excelsior packing around his internal mouth mechanism.

ARMS
The arms are short and relatively straight, with Rexine paw pads. These are now well worn.

His small feet are typical of British bears of this period

Amber eyes attached to long wire shanks

Bear profile *This side view clearly shows the levers in the back of his head, used to open and close his mouth.*

EYES
The ends of the threads holding the large glass eyes are fastened at the back of his head. Some glue has also been used behind the eyes to make them extra secure. Their bulbous nature is slightly reminiscent of the eyes on Merrythought's bear, "Colin" (*see p.54*).

NOSE
The nose at the end of his small, pointed muzzle consists of a rectangular piece of black felt, tightly bound with the original black thread that has faded with age.

Damaged paw reveals cotton

• BEAR ESSENTIALS •

HT: 14in (37cm)

FUR: pale golden-colored, mohair plush
EYES: large, amber, glass, black pupils
EARS: wide, flat, centered over seams of face
MUZZLE: short, blunt; mouth opened by rods

NOSE: wide, rectangular, black felt, thread
ARMS: short; brown Rexine pads; no claws
FEET: small; brown Rexine pads; no claws
STUFFING: cotton; excelsior

DISTINGUISHING FEATURES: The short, straight arms, small feet, and low grade stuffing help identify "Ross" as a postwar British bear.

❧ Jackie-Baby ❧

1953 STEIFF

Jackie-Baby, the Jubilee bear, was produced to celebrate the Steiff teddy bear's 50th birthday. He was designed as a bear cub and was sold in three sizes with an accompanying booklet about the history of the firm. Replicas (also in three sizes) were produced by Steiff in 1986, 1989, and 1990.

EARS
Jackie-Baby has large rounded ears placed along the top and sides of his head.

EYES
He has brown glass eyes on wire shanks, sewn fairly wide apart along the top edge of the muzzle.

TRADEMARK
Jackie-Baby has a 1950s Steiff button and a printed label bearing the manufacturer's name and "US Zone Germany" stitched into his side seam.

FEET
His feet are similar to those belonging to Merrythought's Bingie *(see p.55)*, who is also a bear cub.

Damaged paw reveals excelsior stuffing

Bear profile *Notice Jackie-Baby's large head with its protruding muzzle. His arms are long compared to his stumpy feet.*

NOSE
Jackie-Baby's nose is particularly unusual: a horizontal pink stitch runs across the vertical stitches of dark brown thread.

FUR
Jackie-Baby is made of beige mohair plush; he has a distinct muzzle of clipped plush.

The small dark area represents his navel

• BEAR ESSENTIALS •

HT: 15in (38cm)

FUR: beige, mohair plush; some clipped
EYES: small, brown, glass, wide apart
EARS: rounded, flat, on top and side of head
MUZZLE: large, protruding, clipped plush

NOSE: square; pink and brown stitches
ARMS: long; beige felt pads; claws
FEET: large; beige felt pads; no claws
STUFFING: excelsior throughout bear

Trademark

New style, raised lettering

❧ "Felix" ❧

LATE 1950s DEAN'S RAG BOOK CO. LTD.

"Felix" was the creation of Sylvia R. Wilgoss, chief designer for Dean's from about 1950 until the late 1970s. Part of her successful Tru-to-Life series, this black bear was manufactured in three sizes at the Rye factory in Sussex, England. The company moved from Surrey to Sussex in 1956.

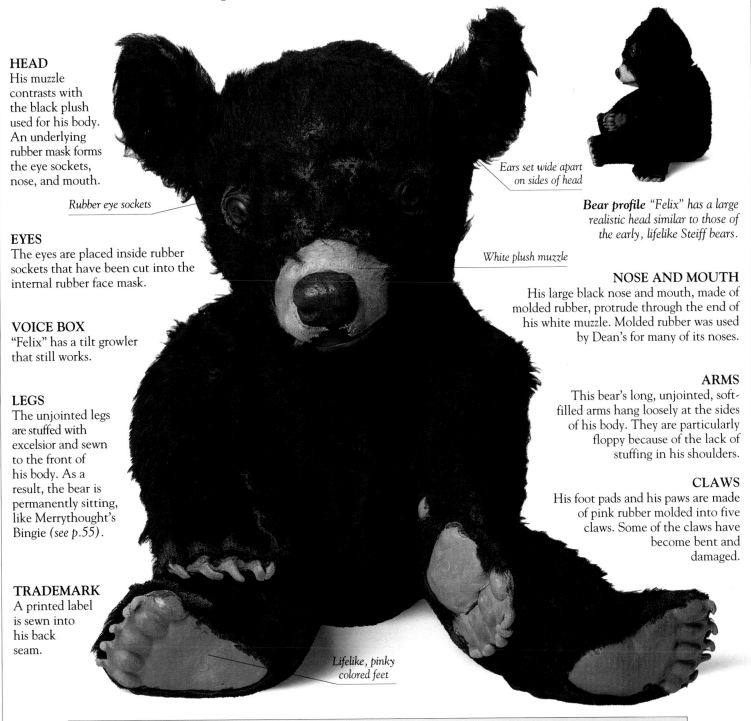

HEAD
His muzzle contrasts with the black plush used for his body. An underlying rubber mask forms the eye sockets, nose, and mouth.

Rubber eye sockets

EYES
The eyes are placed inside rubber sockets that have been cut into the internal rubber face mask.

VOICE BOX
"Felix" has a tilt growler that still works.

LEGS
The unjointed legs are stuffed with excelsior and sewn to the front of his body. As a result, the bear is permanently sitting, like Merrythought's Bingie *(see p.55)*.

TRADEMARK
A printed label is sewn into his back seam.

Ears set wide apart on sides of head

Bear profile *"Felix" has a large realistic head similar to those of the early, lifelike Steiff bears.*

White plush muzzle

NOSE AND MOUTH
His large black nose and mouth, made of molded rubber, protrude through the end of his white muzzle. Molded rubber was used by Dean's for many of its noses.

ARMS
This bear's long, unjointed, soft-filled arms hang loosely at the sides of his body. They are particularly floppy because of the lack of stuffing in his shoulders.

CLAWS
His foot pads and his paws are made of pink rubber molded into five claws. Some of the claws have become bent and damaged.

Lifelike, pinky colored feet

• BEAR ESSENTIALS •

HT: 19in (47cm)

FUR: black-colored, shaggy, acrylic plush
EYES: large, brown glass in rubber sockets
EARS: large, rounded, wide apart in seams
MUZZLE: white acrylic plush

NOSE: molded rubber, large, protruding
ARMS: long; molded rubber pads; claws
FEET: large; molded rubber pads; claws
STUFFING: excelsior and kapok

MADE IN ENGLAND
by Dean's Rag Book CO.LTD
LONDON
Trademark

⇜ "Geoffrey" ⇝
1955 CHAD VALLEY

"Geoffrey" was manufactured during a period of expansion for this already successful British company: in 1938 Chad Valley had received the Royal Warrant of Appointment from the Queen Mother, and so became bear maker to the Royal Family. Originally a family business, Chad Valley became a public company in 1950.

EARS
The bear's wide, flat ears occupy the corners of his head and are set more on the sides of his head than the top.

VOICE BOX
When you tilt the bear, the voice box still works, emitting a high-pitched growl.

The curved arms taper at the shoulders and the paws

FUR
"Geoffrey" has an interesting coat of mixed brown and beige, shaggy mohair plush. The woven backing has a contrasting dark and light weft and warp.

FEET
His feet are small, and the ankles are not very clearly defined.

Bear profile *He has a slightly protruding, but blunt, muzzle and a straight back. Notice how his legs are the same length as his arms.*

Amber glass eyes, with black pupils

NOSE
His long, rectangular nose is typical of the noses on Chad Valley bears. It is composed mainly of vertical stitches.

Hand-embroidered, black thread mouth

TRADEMARK
A printed label on the left foot bears the Royal Warrant. Before 1953 it referred to Queen Elizabeth; after 1953 it changed to the Queen Mother, a point that helps with dating.

Brown Rexine, or oilcloth, foot pads

• BEAR ESSENTIALS •

HT: 16in (40cm)

FUR: brown and beige, shaggy, mohair plush
EYES: medium, amber glass, black pupils
EARS: large, flat, located on sides of head
MUZZLE: blunt and slightly protruding

NOSE: hand-embroidered, rectangular, black
ARMS: curved; brown oilcloth pads; claws
FEET: small; brown oilcloth pads; claws
STUFFING: kapok throughout bear

Royal warrant

Trademark

❧ *Cheeky* ❧

c. 1960 MERRYTHOUGHT

Merrythought's endearing Cheeky design was first registered in 1957. It was produced in a variety of sizes and materials, always with a bell in each of the uniquely large ears. Dressed and open-mouthed Cheekies were also made, as well as Mr. and Mrs. Twisty Cheeky, a dressed couple (see pp.74-75).

EARS
Cheeky's large ears are sewn onto the sides of his head. The front of each ear is made from a darker nylon plush than the back. A metal bell is sandwiched between the pieces of fabric.

EYES
Cheeky has large plastic eyes that lock in for safety. This feature became common in the late 1950s and 1960s (see pp.72-73). The original swing tag would have advertised these safe eyes.

MUZZLE
Cheeky's soft, squishy, velveteen muzzle is London gold, a term used by Merrythought to describe its color.

FEET
His feet are large and extremely wide. The pile on the brown felt pads is slightly worn.

A label bearing the Merrythought trademark is stitched to his foot pad

Bear profile *Cheeky's large, domed head and pert nose are clear from this angle. Notice how his wide smile extends right across the muzzle.*

Curly, honey-colored nylon plush

NOSE AND MOUTH
The tip of the muzzle is tightly bound with black thread to suggest the nose. A cheeky grin embroidered under the nose gives the bear his name.

ARMS
Cheeky's curved arms are short. His shoulders are narrower than his wide, round paws.

The brown felt pads on the paws are circular – an unusual shape

CLAWS
Five relatively short claws are stitched in black thread on each of the foot and paw pads.

• BEAR ESSENTIALS •

HT: 15in (38cm)

FUR: honey-colored, curly, nylon plush
EYES: amber, safe, plastic, black pupils
EARS: large, placed on sides of head
MUZZLE: small, pointed, golden velveteen

NOSE: hand-embroidered, triangular, black
ARMS: wide, round; brown felt pads; claws
FEET: large, wide; brown felt pads; claws
STUFFING: kapok throughout bear

Trademark

❧ "Cully" ❧

c. 1963 WENDY BOSTON PLAYSAFE TOYS LTD.

"Cully" is an excellent example of a machine-washable teddy bear made entirely from synthetic materials. The idea was first introduced by the Wendy Boston firm in 1954. A quarter of the teddy bears exported from Great Britain came from Wendy Boston's Welsh factory before its takeover by Denys Fisher in 1968.

"Cully's" wide ears are from the same piece of fabric as his head

EYES
"Cully" boasts the famous nylon screw-locked eyes patented by Ken and Wendy (*née* Boston) Williams in 1948. The eyes consist of an outer ring of amber-colored plastic and a black pupil made of a molded nylon screw and bolt.

Black thread binds the end of his nose

Bear profile *"Cully" is unjointed and has a fairly flat body – a departure from the traditional teddy bear design.*

Each paw has three claws of black thread

STUFFING
The plastic foam stuffing, a soft and washable material that revolutionized the stuffed toy industry when it was first introduced, has since proved highly toxic if set on fire. It also deteriorates with time.

ARMS
The unjointed arms are short and curved. The way they are attached to his body makes them stretch out in an endearing expression of love.

Shaggy nylon woven plush

LEGS
"Cully" has no clearly defined feet. His legs are straight and stocky, with oval pads of short-pile plush on the ends.

FUR
"Cully" is made from shaggy nylon plush on a woven backing. A short-piled nylon plush is used on his muzzle, foot pads, and paws.

Satin label stitched on right pad

• BEAR ESSENTIALS •

HT: 22in (55cm)

FUR: honey and black, woven-nylon plush
EYES: amber, safe, nylon, black pupils
EARS: large, wide, flat, part of head
MUZZLE: large, short, nylon plush

NOSE: hand-stitched, rectangular, black
ARMS: curved; honey-colored pads; claws
FEET: formless; short-pile pads; no claws
STUFFING: shredded plastic foam

WENDY BOSTON
Made in England
Wash in luke-warm suds

Trademark

❧ "*Bobby Bear*" ❧

c. 1955 PEDIGREE SOFT TOYS LTD.

Pedigree Soft Toys was a subsidiary of Lines Brothers Ltd., once England's largest and most successful toy company. The firm started manufacturing bears in 1937 at Lines' Tri-ang Works in Merton, Surrey; it registered its trademark in 1942. "Bobby Bear" was made at Pedigree's Belfast factory, which opened in 1946.

EARS
The inner edges of each flat ear are folded over. Then the whole ear is sewn into the horizontal seam running along the top of the bear's head.

EYES
His plastic eyes are early examples of the safe lock-in type. A washer behind the fabric probably holds them in place. The amber and black parts appear to be fused together, differentiating them from a Wendy Boston bear's eyes *(see p.84)*.

"Bobby Bear's" red bow is a later embellishment

VOICE BOX
The remains of a squeaker can be felt inside "Bobby Bear's" narrow, excelsior-filled body. It no longer works, though.

The golden mohair plush is well worn

FEET
There is only a slight indication of rounded feet at the ends of the virtually straight, plump legs.

Almost circular pads of beige velveteen show signs of wear and tear

Bear profile *At this angle, it is possible to see "Bobby Bear's" very rounded head with its slight indication of a muzzle. His thin torso, short, straight limbs, and lack of feet are a definite departure from the traditional teddy bear shape.*

Black thread mouth

NOSE
The square-shaped nose is made up of vertical stitches in black thread binding the end of the bear's particularly blunt muzzle.

ARMS
"Bobby Bear's" arms are short and almost straight. They are just slightly curved toward his clawless paws.

STUFFING
"Bobby Bear's" head and body are stuffed with excelsior; his limbs are filled with kapok.

Little remains of the bear's velveteen paw pads

TRADEMARK
A printed fabric label is stitched into "Bobby Bear's" back seam.

• BEAR ESSENTIALS •

HT: 18in (45cm)

FUR: golden-colored, mohair plush
EYES: amber, safe, plastic, black pupils
EARS: medium, flat, edge folded over
MUZZLE: only slightly distinguishable

NOSE: hand-embroidered, square, black
ARMS: curved; velveteen pads; no claws
FEET: barely exist; velveteen pads; no claws
STUFFING: excelsior and kapok mixture

PADDINGTON BEAR

Paddington Bear from Darkest Peru, with his penchant for marmalade, his duffle coat, and his humorous attempts as a kindly but accident-prone foreigner trying to understand the British way of life, has universal appeal. He shot to fame in 1958 when Michael Bond's book *A Bear Called Paddington* was published. The book was a resounding success, and so from 1960 on Michael Bond's stories were published in the United States and translated into numerous languages. In Japan, Paddington is featured on the credit card of the Mitsui Bank.

△ **Bear Boots**
Paddington boots.

THE RISE OF PADDINGTON

Michael Bond based the character on a teddy bear he had bought for his wife from the London store Selfridges in 1956. The bear was later given a duffle coat, hat, and suitcase. He had a book published each year until 1966, and then six new collections of Paddington stories followed between 1968 and 1981. Paperback books came soon after the hardbacks, along with novelties such as pop-up, birthday, and picture books for young readers. Peggy Fortnum's delightful illustrations contributed to the early Paddington's popularity, although other artists, including Fred Banberry, David McKee, and Ivor Wood, have also portrayed the bear. Barry Macey illustrated Paddington's 25th birthday book, written especially for Selfridges in 1983.

WORLDWIDE APPEAL

Paddington Bear stories were featured on British radio and television in the 1960s, and the first musical based on his adventures was performed in both England and Australia in 1973. It was the animated puppet series originally shown on British television in 1975, however, that contributed to the bear's wider following. This was sold to nearly every country in the world and was an international success.

△ **Paddington Man**
Michael Bond, the creator of Paddington Bear, with some of the original illustrations from his books.

△ **Book Illustrations**
Paddington, as drawn by Peggy Fortnum.

▽ **Television Star**
This Paddington puppet from the BBC television series was articulated with steel rods and ball-bearing joints.

△ **Pair of Slippers**
Paddington footwear.

EARLY MERCHANDISING

Paddington wallpaper was available in 1967, but it was not until the 1970s that the merchandising of this bear really expanded. One of the earliest Paddington licensees was Gabrielle Designs, makers of the first stuffed toy Paddington in Britain in 1972; since 1975, New York-based Eden Toys Inc. has held the license for manufacturing stuffed toy Paddingtons throughout the rest of the world. Their bear differed from the British Paddington, in that he had no safety pin in his hat; a pin would have contravened American safety regulations.

FROM BOARD GAMES TO BICYCLE BELLS

Paddington's popularity was so considerable that Michael Bond went on to form Paddington and Co. They were responsible for monitoring the licensing of hundreds of products, ranging from Paddington board games to bicycle bells, and from chocolate to cassettes. In 1978, a store, Paddington and Friends opened in London, dedicated to the internationally famous literary character. A permanent display of Paddington memorabilia can be seen at the London Toy and Model Museum, near Paddington Station. On the concourse of the station, a large bear called Paddington has stood since 1978.

△ *Learning with Paddington*
Paddington enjoying his "elevenses" – the British colloquial term for a mid-morning snack. His books are used abroad to help teach English customs and expressions.

◁ *Bear in Boots*
Shirley Clarkson, of Gabrielle Designs, gave Paddington a pair of wellington boots. Michael Bond later wrote these accessories into the stories. The boots have paw marks and PB written in reverse on the soles.

△ *Paddington's Aunt Lucy*
Gabrielle Designs also created a bear called Aunt Lucy. According to Paddington lore, Aunt Lucy had looked after the young Paddington before his journey to England. She wears traditional Peruvian clothes, including a bowler hat.

❧ "*Joycie*" ❧

c. 1960 JOY TOYS

"Joycie" was made by one of Australia's earliest teddy bear manufacturers. The firm was established by Gerald Kirby and his wife in Melbourne during the late 1920s. A flourishing company making a wide range of stuffed toys, Joy Toys was taken over by the British Lines Brothers in 1966, and eventually disbanded in the late 1970s.

EARS
"Joycie" has small rounded ears placed squarely over the seams of her face. They are stitched into a seam running along the top of her head.

EYES
Her attractive blue glass eyes have metal shanks secured with strong cotton. The cotton is fastened in the middle of her head, at the back.

VOICE BOX
"Joycie" has a squeaker mechanism imported from West Germany. It consists of a round spring encased in soft, clear vinyl; a harder, clear vinyl top contains the reed. The voice box is pushed into a hole cut in the bear's filling.

FEET
The bear's legs are straight and unjointed. Half-circular pieces of mohair plush form the top of her prominent feet.

Oval foot pads are made from the same pale pink synthetic knitted plush as the body

Her muzzle protrudes slightly and is blunt at the end

***Bear profile** The flatness of "Joycie's" completely unjointed body, particularly her all-in-one torso and legs, is evident from this angle.*

Black thread mouth

NOSE
The square nose consists of several vertical stitches of black thread.

Arms point upward very slightly

ARMS
The short, unjointed arms are stitched to the sides of the body and are outstretched in an endearing manner. No paws are indicated.

STUFFING
This Australian bear is made with plastic foam filling, specially molded to fit into the knitted plush skin.

TRADEMARK
A printed label with the manufacturer's name is folded and sewn into the inside seam of the bear's right leg.

• BEAR ESSENTIALS •

HT: 12in (31cm)

FUR: pale pink, synthetic knitted plush
EYES: medium-sized, blue, glass, black pupils
EARS: small, rounded, square over face seams
MUZZLE: blunt and slightly protruding

NOSE: hand-embroidered, square, black
ARMS: no paws indicated; no pads; no claws
FEET: prominent, plush pads, no claws
STUFFING: plastic foam cut to body shape

Trademark

❧ "Leon" ❧

1962 H.G. STONE & CO. LTD.

"Leon," another Hugmee bear (see p.67), was manufactured at H.G. Stone's Pontypool factory in Wales. He was made shortly before the death of Leon Rees, one of the company's founders. In 1964, H.G. Stone was taken over by Dunbee-Combex-Marx, a British company, manufacturing vinyl dolls and toys.

VOICE BOX
A round squeaker, probably of the kind that uses cardboard, a spring, and oilcloth (*see p.73*), can be felt inside "Leon's" rounded body. It is still working.

Safe, lock-in eyes made of amber and brown plastic

Honey-colored mohair plush

Thin black embroidery-silk mouth

Bear profile *From the side, you can see "Leon's" typical Chiltern flat-backed head, with its extensive forehead and slightly protruding muzzle.*

FEET
"Leon's" large feet have long, pointed, velveteen pads, reinforced with cardboard. Similar Chiltern bears with oilcloth pads date from an earlier period.

Despite H.G. Stone's move to Pontypool, the company still maintained the Chiltern name for its bears

NOSE
The shape of "Leon's" small nose resembles a heraldic shield. The nose consists of vertical stitches of thin black embroidery silk. Chiltern bears of this period also had molded plastic noses, although the company finally reverted back to stitching, preferring the traditional method.

ARMS
The arms are longer than the legs, but are tapered, with very wide shoulders. They are curved in the usual way.

CLAWS
"Leon" has five claws stitched on the plush of each foot. He has only four claws on his paws. These run from the pad onto the plush.

TRADEMARK
A printed label is stitched to "Leon's" left side seam under his arm. He also has a printed cardboard swing tag, noting that he was "Awarded the Certificate of the Royal Institute of Public Health and Hygiene."

The thread used for the claws is double thickness

• BEAR ESSENTIALS •

HT: 21in (53cm)

FUR: honey-colored, mohair plush
EYES: amber, safe, plastic, black pupils
EARS: long, narrow, gathered at base
MUZZLE: blunt, slightly protruding, rounded

NOSE: hand-stitched shieldlike, black
ARMS: curved; beige velveteen pads; claws
FEET: large; beige velveteen pads; claws
STUFFING: kapok and excelsior

THE TEDDY COMES OF AGE

A number of people and events at the end of the 1960s and early 1970s had a lasting impact on the development of the teddy bear. The publication of The Teddy Bear Book by the British actor Peter Bull, in 1969, was the main precursor of what was to become an international arctophily movement. The book not only surveyed, almost for the first time, the teddy bear's history – his origins and the developments of the teddy bear manufacturing industry – but also considered the toy's unique relationship with his or her owner and its significance in that person's life.

THE TEDDY BEAR RENAISSANCE

The new awareness of bears was further fueled by the various teddy bear books and events coming out of the International Year of the Child in 1979. Together with the work of Good Bears of the World, an organization providing needy children with teddy bears, they succeeded in bringing together many like-minded people. About this time there was a teddy bear renaissance, a mania similar to that of the early years. This time, however, it was more remarkable because of multimedia coverage and technological advancements.

△ **Hands**
Applause was once a division of the famous Knickerbocker Toy Co.

CHANGING HANDS

The new wave of nostalgia, the public's greater awareness of its heritage, and the value of craftsmanship encouraged the establishment of cottage industries producing handmade, traditionally designed teddy bears from a combination of natural and modern materials. The worldwide economic recession of the 1970s led to the downfall of many of the major teddy bear manufacturers by the 1980s. For example, products belonging to the British firm Palitoy, which owned the Chad Valley label, and Pedigree Soft Toys Ltd. were lost to the American Hasbro (originally the Hassenfield Brothers Inc.) which was destined to become a world leader in the toy field. Such multinational companies now play an important role in teddy manufacture.

△ **Bear Artist**
The trademark of well-known American bear artist Mac Pohlen based in California.

△ **Santa Claus**
A miniature teddy bear dressed as Santa Claus, made by American bear artist Linda Kuch.

▽ **Peter Bull**
Actor Peter Bull was also author of The Teddy Bear Book and A Hug of Teddy Bears.

NEW STANDARD OF SAFETY

Regulations regarding the physical, flammable, and toxicological properties of toys were constantly updated. In 1989, a Lion mark was introduced to indicate to shoppers which toys conformed to current British standards. Despite earlier breakthroughs on bear washability, many teddies were made carrying instructions to "surface wash only."

△ **Bejeweled Bear**
The romantic author Barbara Cartland once owned this bear, now at the Teddy Bear Museum in Stratford-upon-Avon, England.

△ American Creation
This bear is the work of the contemporary American bear artist Ginger T. Brame.

TEDDY BEAR ARTISTS

The late 1970s saw a number of individuals setting themselves up as teddy bear artists, a phenomenon at first peculiar to the United States, and it spread worldwide during the 1980s. The leadership of this movement includes such names as Dee Hockenberry *(see p.113)*, Beverly Wright, Flore Emory, and Doris and Terry Michaud. These artists designed and hand-made bears, often based on the traditional style, in limited editions. Several artists chose to exaggerate the basic form. Ballard Baines and Linda Spiegel, for example, made rather unnatural-looking creatures with thin, bent limbs. Other artists used nontraditional materials: In America, Beverly Port designed porcelain-faced bears, and the creations of Robert Raikes had wooden faces *(see p.109)*.

IMAGINATIONS RUN WILD

Some of the larger firms began to use unconventional fabrics. The North American Bear Co.'s brightly colored VIB's *(see pp.94-95)* and Gabrielle Design's terry cloth bears are examples. Imaginations began to run wild as personalities, vampires, Indian squaws, Santa Claus, and Santa Lucia themes were applied to the modern bear. The ultimate in these bears are the bears in disguise, such as Bev Miller's Bunny Bear, while Flore Emory and Ginger T. Brame have produced Bumble Bears, with striped plush bodies, wings, and antennae. Teddy bears had reached art form status when Kimberlee Port's green plush Christmas Tree Bear, covered with decorations, was exhibited in a New York gallery in 1987.

LUXURY ITEMS

These sophisticated personality bears were produced for adults, rather than children. They were designed as luxury accessories, the ultimate example being the expensive mink teddy bear available at London's Fortnum and Mason store in 1980. Some bears are designed as collectors' pieces, and capture the elongated features used by the earlier teddy designers. The bears of Naomi Laight *(see p.108)* and Susan Rixon *(see p.111)* are cases in point. Some artists reverted to the use of traditional shoe buttons or glass eyes. If such eyes are used, the toys have a tag reading, "This is not a child's toy."

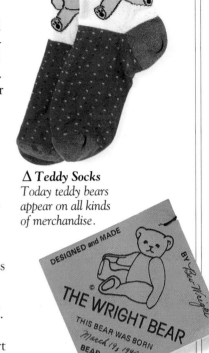

△ Teddy Socks
Today teddy bears appear on all kinds of merchandise.

△ Happy Birthday
American bear artist Bev Wright's teddies have their birthdays written on cardboard swing tags.

▽ American Artists' Work
The creations of some contemporary American bear artists.

△ Speed Mascot
Gina Campbell, daughter of Donald Campbell, waterspeed record breaker, attempting to set a new record in 1984 with her father's mascot.

◁ Oriental Accessory
A teddy bear paper garland made in Taiwan for the American market.

BEAR NECESSITIES

I n recent years two types of teddy bears have emerged. Some manufacturers are making an unjointed, cuddly creature from safe, all-synthetic, fully-washable materials for children. Others aim for the collectors' market and, using natural materials such as mohair plush, make traditional jointed bears with long limbs, muzzles, and humped backs. Teddy bears that can walk and talk, with the help of microchips installed in their bodies, are also being produced.

JOINTS
Molded plastic all-in-one disks and pins have been introduced.

  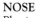

Safe plastic eye with metal washer

Plastic shoe button eyes

NOSE
Plastic molded noses are either realistic or stylized. They are usually secured with a washer.

SHOE BUTTON EYES
Replica shoe button eyes, copying the traditional designs on early bears, are secured with washers in the safe, modern way.

Plastic cover   *Metal washer*

PLASTIC EYES
Safe, lock-in plastic eyes come in a wide variety of sizes and colors. They are held in place with metal washers that occasionally have additional plastic covers for extra security.

FABRIC
Teddies destined to be children's toys are made with artificial plush fabrics. There is, nevertheless, a marked move toward natural fibers, like mohair, for bears aimed at the collectors' market. "Distressed" mohair, which is treated to appear old, was introduced in the mid-1980s.

Woven mohair plush

Half mohair, half wool, on cotton backing

Distressed mohair plush

Cotton thread   *Nylon thread*

MACHINE-STITCHING
The separate parts of a bear are machine-stitched together with cotton or synthetic thread. Clear nylon has become popular, since it is both strong and invisible.

Shredded plastic foam

Excelsior

Acrylic plush on knitted backing

Plastic frame for small bear

MINIBEARS
Tiny bears have molded plastic frames, with swivel-jointed limbs and heads.

DETAILS
Embroidery thread is still popular for the task of hand-stitching noses, mouths, and claws, but wool is also used.

Wool *Embroidery thread*

Draylon
Synthetic plush

PAD FABRICS
Artificial fabrics, such as Draylon, are widely used, but the makers of traditional bears prefer real suede or chamois leather.

Colored felts

Ultrasuede

Suede

Japanese music box with clear plastic lid

MUSIC BOXES
Encased in plastic since the 1960s, the Swiss clockwork movement mechanism (*see p.37*) is now made by Japanese firms.

Plastic flat squeaker

Plastic concertina squeaker

Reed

Plastic tube for reed

TILT GROWLER
The weight and bellows are now contained in a plastic canister. The growl comes through a perforated speaker.

SQUEAKER
Squeakers are made of thin molded plastic and are either flat or a concertina shape. Both have metal and plastic reeds, protected by a plastic tube.

Perforated speaker

Polyester wadding

1988 APPLAUSE
Made in California, this unjointed bear is filled with polyester stuffing. His plush is artificial, he has lock-in plastic, replica shoe button eyes, a lock-in plastic nose, and a stitched mouth.

Plastic foam and polystyrene pellet mix

Low-grade cotton waste

STUFFING
Excelsior is favored, particularly for the heads of collectors' bears. As plastic foam pieces and polystyrene pellets used in the 1950s and 1960s were found to crumble and to give off toxic fumes in the event of fire, polyester wadding came into its own in the 1970s. Low-grade cotton waste is still used for cheap bears.

BEAR APPAREL

With renewed bullishness for bears and the return of the traditional, jointed, teddy-doll shape in the 1970s, bears with closets full of clothes came back into fashion. The inventiveness that had been lacking since before World War II returned with a vengeance as each manufacturer tried to tempt the collector with yet another bear in disguise. Teddy bears, it seemed, could no longer remain just bare bears. They had to be employed in every kind of occupation that could give rise to an outfit easily worn by an upright, furry animal. In the United States, in particular, the imagination of some manufacturers ran wild. These designer bears are, however, for the affluent buyer.

△ **Biggles Bear**
An airport souvenir made in the 1980s.

UNIFORMED BEARS

The 1970s were difficult years for the toy industry, yet, despite this, several manufacturers produced novelty bears in costume. Steiff's 1972 Hockey Teddy had a numbered blue plush jersey that was all-in-one with his body and limbs. Merrythought continued the tradition of the masculine, uniformed teddy with its Beefeater, Policeman, Guardsman, and Highlander Bears. These were first produced in the early 1970s and they were later reintroduced in the 1980s. Meanwhile, the 20th birthday of its successful Cheeky bear (see p.83) in 1977 was celebrated with the launch of Bedtime Bear, sporting pajamas and a bright red bathrobe. The Chicago-based North American Bear Co.'s range of famous historical figures included Napoleon Bearnaparte and the Statue of Libearty. Sports bears, such as Hermann's Golfer with his plaid plus fours and cap, and golf clubs, were particularly popular. Bocs Teganau has made a bear dressed as Geoffrey Boycott, the famous British cricketer; he wears his full cricket uniform, and holds a miniature V12 Slazenger bat.

◁ **Back to School**
This schoolboy bear with his leather satchel was made in a limited edition of 100 bears by the British company Dormouse Designs in 1989.

△ Sailor Bear
A limited edition Bob Raikes bear made in 1985.

DESIGNER OUTFITS

As in the period of teddy bear mania at the beginning of the century, various manufacturers attempted to meet the growing demand for individual outfits. The North American Bear Co. produced the Vander Bear Family who came with a variety of outfits and accessories which collectors could acquire, such as the Musical Soiree and the Victorian Sleep Wear sets. In Britain, small firms followed suit. The Sussex-based Bear Wear Co., for example, produced limited edition, designer, hand-knitted sweaters and other unique outfits. A line of bears known as the Sloane Ranger Bears (named after a particular social clique who lived around Sloane Square in London) was produced in England. These bears wore appropriate Sloane Ranger outfits, such as snappy ski togs and stylish jackets for the country. British walkers were also parodied in the English Lakeland Bears series; the bears wore traditional walking gear and hand-made clogs. However, as always, children today are still likely to practice their first hesitant "knit one, purl one" on teddy's new scarf or sweater, so there are still plenty of homemade clothes around.

△ Star Struck
Humphrey Beargart was made by the North American Bear Co.

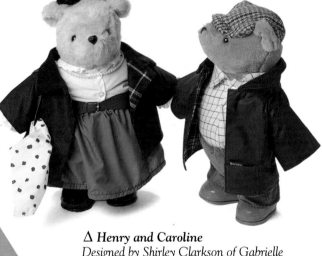

△ Henry and Caroline
Designed by Shirley Clarkson of Gabrielle Designs, Henry and Caroline are part of her Sloane Ranger line representing young upwardly mobile professionals, also known as yuppies.

◁ Here Comes The Bride
The lovely bride and groom were reproduced by the Franklin Mint in the late 1980s. They are based on teddy bears in the collection of the late Colonel Bob Henderson (see pp.122-123).

BEAR MEMORABILIA

The teddy bear craze that had taken the world by storm at the beginning of the century returned with even more vigor in its latter years. Manufacturers competed with each other to meet the demands of the dedicated arctophile, providing him or her with every conceivable teddy-inspired accessory – from jewelry, ornaments, clothing, and household items, to refrigerator magnets, telephones, and car alarms. There was also renewed interest in miniature bears (which had been common in the 1930s), and this was helped by the simultaneous rise in popularity of dolls' houses and miniature collecting. As a result of the technological advances in the electronics industry, several talking bears appeared on the international market in the mid-1980s.

△ Teddy Lapel Pin
This pin was made in 1984 by Steiff.

TELEVISION STARS

The success of merchandising television characters like Paddington in the early 1970s *(see p.86-87)* inspired others to follow suit. The most notable in the teddy bear world were Super Ted and, later, Tough Ted, who were both originally characters in children's books. Tough Ted, created by Simon Bond, was an ex-Merchant Navy seabear who ran a seaside café. After appearing on television, he was reproduced as a stuffed toy by Golden Bear Products, complete with a torn ear, five o'clock shadow, and embroidered tattoos.

◁ Super Ted
Super Ted – the creation of Mike Young – was originally a children's book character. He was featured in a highly successful animated cartoon series, shown worldwide on television in the 1980s. This version was produced in the United States.

◁ Teddy in School
This little ted was made by the contemporary bear artist Elaine Fujita-Gamble. He has his own desk, books, and an apple for his lunch.

▷ Teddy Ruxpin
First produced in 1984 by the giant toy company Mattel, Teddy Ruxpin can talk with the aid of a story-telling cassette.

THE ULTIMATE BEAR GIMMICK

Manufacturers are constantly striving to create the ultimate teddy bear novelty. The production of miniature teddy bears has become a serious art form. In the United States, artists such as Elaine Fujita-Gamble, Dickie Harrison, Linda Kuch, and Laurie Sasaki produce highly collectible miniature bears, while in England, the tiny teddies of Anita Oliver, some only one inch high, are prized. Each bear is traditionally jointed, hand-sewn, and stuffed with kapok. Miniature teddy bears are also produced in ceramic, silver, pewter, crystal, and modern synthetic materials. Especially unusual are those made out of moss or fresh bread.

The ultimate is, perhaps, Mr. Bills, produced in 1987 from clear plastic and stuffed with $250,000 worth of shredded bills. With the development of the microchip, manufacturers attempted to create a teddy bear with a realistic speaking mechanism. Hasbro's Bingo Bear has a 400-word vocabulary that he puts to use when he is cuddled or his chin is scratched. Mattel's Teddy Ruxpin blinks, wriggles his nose, and opens and shuts his mouth in perfect synchronization with his voice which is on a specially recorded story-telling cassette.

△ **Muff and Purse Bear**
This muff and purse bear was made by Merrythought in the 1980s.

△ **Ted-in-the-Box**
This tiny ted is just the size of a postage stamp.

▽ **Bear Chair**
A child's chair made of pine by the British firm Bear Essentials.

◁ **Money Bear**
Bear artist Sue E. Foskey made this money bear in 1987. When you put down the flap of the bag, the bear growls.

▷ **Fozzie Bear**
The original Fozzie Bear, now in a museum in England, was designed by the late Jim Henson, creator of the Muppets.

❧ "Darren" ❧

1975 PEDIGREE SOFT TOYS LTD.

"Darren" was manufactured in Canterbury, England, where Pedigree was based throughout the 1970s and 1980s, until its eventual collapse in 1988. In 1966, the firm merged with Rovex Industries Ltd., a subsidiary of the Lines Brothers Group. Both companies were taken over by Dunbee-Combex-Marx in 1972.

EARS
The bear's very large ears are flat and narrow. They are sewn more onto the sides than onto the top of his large head.

EYES
His safe, lock-in eyes are made of amber and black plastic, and they are positioned just inside each face seam.

VOICE BOX
"Darren's" rounded body houses a modern plastic tilt growler. The original box in which he was sold advertised "I growl."

Thin, black, stitched mouth

FEET
The stumpy feet have irregularly shaped oval pads made from dark brown synthetic velvet. There is no indication of claws.

TRADEMARK
A printed satin label bearing the manufacturer's name is folded over and stitched into the lower part of the bear's back seam.

Bear profile At this angle, the bear's large head and ears, his small, rounded, slightly protruding muzzle and short, stumpy limbs are clear.

Clipped nylon plush with a woven backing

NOSE
"Darren" has a molded black plastic nose, reminiscent of a dog's. It is secured on the end of his muzzle with a washer.

The ribbon is original

ARMS
The upward-curving arms are the same length as the legs. They are wider in the centers than at the shoulders and paws.

Golden-colored flame-resistant plush with a knitted backing

• BEAR ESSENTIALS •

HT: 16in (40cm)

FUR: golden, flame-resistant nylon plush
EYES: amber, safe, plastic, black pupils
EARS: large, wide, flat, on sides of head
MUZZLE: protruding, clipped nylon plush

NOSE: molded plastic, doglike, black
ARMS: short; brown synthetic pads; no claws
FEET: stumpy; brown synthetic pads; no claws
STUFFING: shredded plastic foam

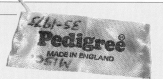

"Trayton"

1976 MERRYTHOUGHT LTD.

Merrythought manufactured a series of traditional teddy bears from 1965 until 1985. They were made in nine sizes; this example, the smallest, was introduced in 1975. Before World War II all the plush came from mills in Yorkshire, England, but the mohair now used by Merrythought is largely imported, often from the Far East.

EYES
His small amber and black plastic eyes are the safe lock-in type. They are set low down, giving him a high forehead, a feature typical of later British bears.

ARMS
"Trayton's" short arms are tapered, with thin paws curving upward. The synthetic pads are brown.

The mohair plush is a color Merrythought described as London gold

FEET
"Trayton's" very small feet are barely distinguishable from his legs. The brown knitted synthetic pads are irregular in shape.

Large, flat ears positioned across face seams

Bear profile *"Trayton" is a typical late British bear with a flat, rounded muzzle, arms and legs of the same length, almost nonexistent feet, and a thin, straight body.*

An inverted V-shaped mouth

NOSE
The almost round nose is embroidered with black, mainly vertical stitches, with a few horizontal ones on top.

The flamboyant red bow is original

TRADEMARK
"Trayton" has a printed label on his right foot and a printed cardboard swing tag.

• BEAR ESSENTIALS •

FUR: London gold, pure mohair plush
EYES: amber, safe, plastic, black pupils
EARS: large, flat, squarely across face seams
MUZZLE: blunt, rounded, slightly protruding

NOSE: hand-embroidered, rounded, black
ARMS: short; synthetic pads; no claws
FEET: small; synthetic pads; no claws
STUFFING: kapok; excelsior in muzzle

HT: 10in (25cm)

Trademark

❧ "*Brummy*" ☙

1977 CHILTERN/CHAD VALLEY

In 1967, Chiltern Soft Toys became a subsidiary of Chad Valley, creating England's largest stuffed toy manufacturer. Ten years later, "Brummy" was produced in Birmingham. In 1978, Chad Valley was bought by the nearby Leicester firm Palitoy, which in turn was taken over by the American company Kenner Parker in the 1980s.

EARS
"Brummy's" large and rounded, flat ears are stitched squarely over his facial seams.

EYES
His plastic eyes are amber and black. They are the safe lock-in type used by most manufacturers of the time.

Slightly protruding muzzle

VOICE BOX
A red plastic concertina squeaker (*see pp.92-93*) is embedded in "Brummy's" body.

Golden-colored, luxury mohair plush

FEET
"Brummy's" small feet have tear-shaped pads of a brown synthetic knit. He has no claws as is often the case with British bears made in this period.

Bear profile *This view reveals the flatness of his design, his thin body, small head, and uniformly short limbs.*

Black thread mouth

NOSE
"Brummy's" small, almost square nose is hand-stitched in black thread. It is more like the noses of early Chiltern teddies than the easily recognizable long, thick noses found on Chad Valley bears.

Original orange bow

TRADEMARK
The names Chad Valley and Chiltern are printed with the Royal Warrant on a cardboard swing tag. The Royal Warrant was granted to Chad Valley in 1938.

ARMS
The bear's short arms are the same length as his legs. They have a slight curve and the paw ends are hooked.

• BEAR ESSENTIALS •

HT: 12in (30cm)

FUR: golden-colored, luxury mohair plush
EYES: amber, safe, plastic, black pupils
EARS: rounded, flat, square over face seams
MUZZLE: blunt and slightly protruding

NOSE: hand-embroidered, squarish, black
ARMS: short; brown synthetic pads; no claws
FEET: small; brown synthetic pads; no claws
STUFFING: colored, synthetic fabric waste

Trademark

❧ Bigo Bello ❧

c. 1970 SCHREYER & CO.

Bigo Bello was one of a Schuco series of plush toys made to be bent into a variety of positions. This bear also talks when a cord is pulled out from his side. The patented toys were produced from the 1960s until the firm was taken over in 1976 by Dunbee-Combex-Marx, one of Europe's leading toy manufacturers.

EARS
The bear's flat ears create a slight curve. They are placed squarely over the seams of his face.

EYES
The clear glass eyes with brown painted backs and black pupils are typically Schuco. They are secured with hooked wire shanks.

VOICE BOX
Bigo Bello's excelsior-filled stomach contains a mechanism commonly used as early as the late 1950s. When the cord at the side of the bear is pulled, a miniature record inside a protective plastic box plays eight German phrases. Translated, they include "Hello, Mommy," "My name is Bigo Bello," and "Give me a kiss."

Cream clipped rayon plush pads with no claws

LIMBS
Bigo Bello is unjointed, but a flexible wire armature in his limbs makes it possible to bend him into a variety of positions.

Long brown artificial silk plush on a woven backing

Flexible soft-filled legs and arms

Bear profile *Bigo Bello has a rounded stomach and straight, unjointed legs. From this angle, you can see the plastic ring that activates his voice.*

Single black vertical stitch extending from nose to mouth

NOSE AND MUZZLE
His black nose is made from hard vinyl. It is glued to a muzzle made from the same clipped artificial silk plush as the foot and paw pads.

Printed cardboard tag and cream ribbon attached to chest

MOUTH
This Schuco bear has an open mouth similar to that of his older cousin, "Heinrich" *(see p.59)*. Bigo Bello's mouth, however, is lined with pink felt, and he has a tongue represented by a smudge of red paint. The edge of the jaw is defined by a thin line of brown paint.

• BEAR ESSENTIALS •

HT: 16in (40cm)

FUR: brown, long, artificial silk plush
EYES: medium, glass, brown painted backs
EARS: small, slightly curved, over face seams
MUZZLE: clipped artificial silk plush

NOSE: smooth, molded vinyl, oval, black
ARMS: unjointed; cream rayon pads; no claws
FEET: large; cream rayon pads; no claws
STUFFING: excelsior; soft-filled

Trademark

❧ Bully Bear ❧

1981 THE HOUSE OF NISBET LTD.

The House of Nisbet started in 1953 as a doll-making business, but in 1978 it began making teddy bears for the collectors' market. Alison Wilson, daughter of the founder, designed Bully Bear for its Nisbet Childhood Classics line, drawing inspiration from a bear belonging to the late Peter Bull, the English actor and bear collector.

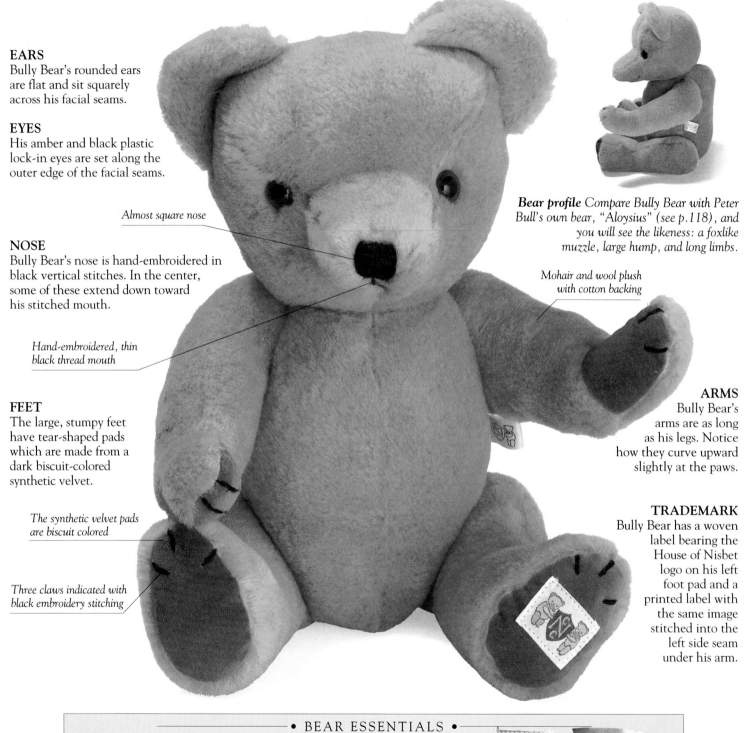

EARS
Bully Bear's rounded ears are flat and sit squarely across his facial seams.

EYES
His amber and black plastic lock-in eyes are set along the outer edge of the facial seams.

Almost square nose

NOSE
Bully Bear's nose is hand-embroidered in black vertical stitches. In the center, some of these extend down toward his stitched mouth.

Hand-embroidered, thin black thread mouth

FEET
The large, stumpy feet have tear-shaped pads which are made from a dark biscuit-colored synthetic velvet.

The synthetic velvet pads are biscuit colored

Three claws indicated with black embroidery stitching

Bear profile *Compare Bully Bear with Peter Bull's own bear, "Aloysius" (see p.118), and you will see the likeness: a foxlike muzzle, large hump, and long limbs.*

Mohair and wool plush with cotton backing

ARMS
Bully Bear's arms are as long as his legs. Notice how they curve upward slightly at the paws.

TRADEMARK
Bully Bear has a woven label bearing the House of Nisbet logo on his left foot pad and a printed label with the same image stitched into the left side seam under his arm.

• BEAR ESSENTIALS •

HT: 18in (45cm)

FUR: golden, mohair and wool plush
EYES: amber, safe, plastic, black pupils
EARS: medium, rounded, flat, sit squarely
MUZZLE: very long and pointed, foxlike

NOSE: hand-embroidered, squarish, black
ARMS: curved; biscuit synthetic pads; claws
FEET: large; biscuit synthetic pads; claws
STUFFING: synthetic

Trademark

❧ *Flash* ❧

1980 CANTERBURY BEARS

Flash was the first bear manufactured by this family business, established in 1980. From their home in Canterbury, England, John and Maude Blackburn and their three children still produce a variety of traditional teddy bears as well as special commissions for export around the world. (Replicas of Flash are available.)

EARS
Flash's peculiarly large and floppy ears hang from the sides of his head, similar to those of the 1930s "Miss Jessie Criddle" *(see p.60).*

Old-fashioned spectacles

ARMS
His relatively short, fat arms only taper slightly toward the paws.

Huge, plastic lock-in amber eyes

FUR
The fur is long, light brown man-made fabric with a knit backing. (The plush on replicas has a woven backing.)

FEET
Flash's large feet and narrow pads are similar to the ones found on early bears.

Cream chamois leather pads

Bear profile *Seen from the side, Flash's extraordinarily long, floppy ears make him more reminiscent of a dog than a bear.*

Protruding but blunt muzzle

NOSE
The molded plastic nose is more like the type used on 1950s bears than the hand-embroidered detail of the early traditional models.

ACCESSORIES
Flash proudly wears a row of six British medals from the two World Wars and an American medal given to him at a teddy bear show held in California. His spectacles enhance his distinguished appearance.

• BEAR ESSENTIALS •

FUR: light brown, long, artificial plush
EYES: large, amber, safe, plastic, black pupils
EARS: large, floppy, hang from sides of head
MUZZLE: large, blunt and protruding
HT: 33in (84cm)

NOSE: molded plastic, realistic, black
ARMS: thick; cream leather pads; no claws
FEET: large; cream leather pads; no claws
STUFFING: synthetic

❧ *"Johann"* ❧

c. 1970 GEBRUDER HERMANN

"Johann" is one of thousands of fine quality, handmade teddy bears exported by this successful German toy manufacturer. Since the 1960s Gebrüder Hermann has been led by the three Hermann brothers, Artur, Werner, and Hellmuth, grandsons of the founder.

EARS
"Johann" has particularly small, flat ears, which are positioned squarely over the seams of his face.

EYES
The amber and black glass eyes are attached to the bear's face with wire shanks. They are positioned on the outside of the facial seams and the edge of the muzzle.

Clipped mohair plush on muzzle

TRADEMARK
The Hermann metal tag is always attached to the bear's chest with a red cord, but its design has changed over the years – a helpful clue to a bear's date.

Long mohair plush

FEET
His feet are very small, and his ankles are not well defined. The tear-shaped pads are made from pinky colored felt and match those on his paws.

Bear profile "Johann's" long, protruding muzzle, straight back, short arms, and small feet distinguish him from traditional teddy bears.

NOSE AND MOUTH
The thin, lozenge-shaped nose at the end of the muzzle consists of a few horizontal stitches in black thread. A vertical stitch extends from his nose to his inverted V-shaped mouth.

Three distinctive black thread claws on both paws and feet

ARMS
The short, tapering arms have thick shoulders and thin paws that curve slightly upward.

• BEAR ESSENTIALS •

HT: 19in (48cm)

FUR: golden, mohair plush; some clipped
EYES: medium, amber, glass, black pupils
EARS: small, flat, squarely over face seams
MUZZLE: protuding, clipped mohair plush

NOSE: hand-embroidered, black
ARMS: short; pinky colored felt pads; claws
FEET: small; pinky colored felt pads; claws
STUFFING: excelsior throughout bear

Trademark

❧ *Original Teddy* ❧
1990 STEIFF

Every few years, Steiff creates a modern version of one of its original bears. Petsy, Molly, and Zotty have all been honored in this way. The descriptively named Original Teddy bears, based on Steiff's 1905 bear, have been made in various colors and sizes, and have been one of the company's most popular lines for more than 20 years.

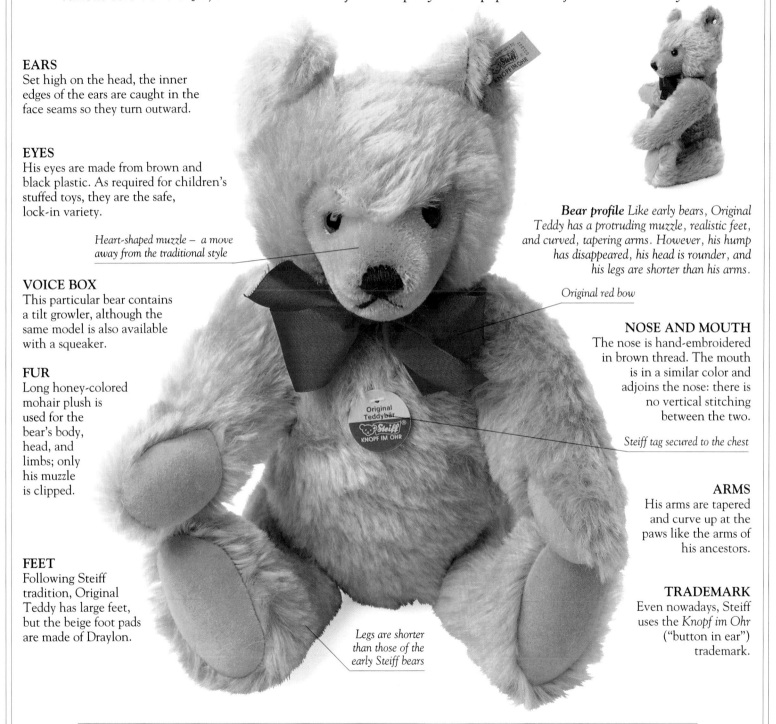

EARS
Set high on the head, the inner edges of the ears are caught in the face seams so they turn outward.

EYES
His eyes are made from brown and black plastic. As required for children's stuffed toys, they are the safe, lock-in variety.

Heart-shaped muzzle – a move away from the traditional style

VOICE BOX
This particular bear contains a tilt growler, although the same model is also available with a squeaker.

FUR
Long honey-colored mohair plush is used for the bear's body, head, and limbs; only his muzzle is clipped.

FEET
Following Steiff tradition, Original Teddy has large feet, but the beige foot pads are made of Draylon.

Bear profile *Like early bears, Original Teddy has a protruding muzzle, realistic feet, and curved, tapering arms. However, his hump has disappeared, his head is rounder, and his legs are shorter than his arms.*

Original red bow

NOSE AND MOUTH
The nose is hand-embroidered in brown thread. The mouth is in a similar color and adjoins the nose: there is no vertical stitching between the two.

Steiff tag secured to the chest

ARMS
His arms are tapered and curve up at the paws like the arms of his ancestors.

TRADEMARK
Even nowadays, Steiff uses the *Knopf im Ohr* ("button in ear") trademark.

Legs are shorter than those of the early Steiff bears

• BEAR ESSENTIALS •

HT: 14in (36cm)

FUR: honey-colored, long, mohair plush
EYES: brown, safe, plastic, black pupils
EARS: small, outward-turning, high on head ·
MUZZLE: protruding, clipped mohair plush

NOSE: hand-embroidered, oval, brown
ARMS: long; beige Draylon pads; no claws
FEET: large; beige Draylon pads; no claws
STUFFING: synthetic wadding

Made in Germany by Steiff ®
KNOPF IM OHR
0201/51
Trademark

❧ "Michael" ❧

1987 DEAN'S CO. (1903) LTD.

*An international takeover in 1986 gave Dean's Rag Book Co. Ltd. a new name: Dean's Co. (1903) Ltd.
In 1990, however, the company revived its old name and launched a new line of reproduction bears. The firm still
operates from Pontypool in Wales, where it has been based since 1974.*

EARS
"Michael" has small, flat ears. The inner edges of each ear are caught in the facial seams; the rest is placed on the side of his head.

Safe, lock-in eyes made from amber and black plastic

ACCESSORIES
"Michael" is sold with a stylish red ribbon tied around his neck. He comes in a printed calico bag with a drawstring, instead of a box.

Stitched U-shaped mouth

London gold wool and mohair plush

FEET
His feet are relatively long and wide. The narrow oval pads are made of brown synthetic velveteen.

Short stumpy legs and big feet

Bear profile "Michael" has a rounded head and protruding muzzle. Notice his unusually square shoulders, short legs, and arms with hooked paws.

Muzzle made from a separate piece of fabric to the head

NOSE
The nose is embroidered in black thread to form a triangular shape. No vertical stitching joins the nose with the mouth.

ARMS
The tapered arms are particularly short with narrow, almost hooklike, paws. The pads match those on his feet.

TRADEMARK
A woven, folded label showing the company's new name is sewn into the side seam under the left arm. A folded, printed card (not visible here) is sewn into his left ear.

• BEAR ESSENTIALS •

HT: 19in (48cm)

FUR: London gold, wool and mohair plush
EYES: amber, safe, plastic, black pupils
EARS: small, flat, placed wide apart
MUZZLE: protruding, separate fabric piece

NOSE: hand-embroidered, triangular, black
ARMS: short; brown synthetic pads; no claws
FEET: wide; brown synthetic pads; no claws
STUFFING: polyurethane foam granules

Trademark

❧ "Watty Watford" ❧

1982 R. DAKIN & CO.

"Watty Watford," a Woolie Bear, was produced by R. Dakin & Co. in San Francisco as part of a line of bears. Founded in 1955, the firm originally imported toys, along with other products. It was not until the 1970s that Dakin established itself as a stuffed toy manufacturer.

EYES
His clear plastic eyes, with brown backs and black pupils, are safely locked into the fabric with washers that pass through the face seams. Dakin is renowned for its high safety standards, so the eyes would have undergone rigorous stress tests, probably more demanding than those dictated by government safety regulations.

A very round, bulbous head

EARS
The small ears are wide and narrow. They are secured to the sides of his head.

Unjointed arms hang straight down the sides of the body

TRADEMARK
A folded fabric label sewn into the back seam gives details on the materials used to make the bear. He also has a swing tag secured to his neck.

At the paw ends, the arms are slightly wider

FEET
When his socks are removed, his feet reveal wide, pear-shaped pads made from the same material as the rest of his body – white wool pile on a polyester backing.

The muzzle occupies the entire face

Bear profile *"Watty Watford" has straight, unjointed arms and legs. His legs are sewn to the front of his body, so he is permanently sitting.*

Hand-embroidered, brown wool mouth

NOSE
Hand-embroidered vertical stitches in brown wool form a triangle at the point where the two face seams join at the muzzle.

FUR
"Watty Watford" is made from a white plush material, consisting of a short wool pile on a polyester machine-knitted backing. The Woolie Bear range was also available in a gold plush.

ACCESSORIES
"Watty Watford" wears a striped scarf and socks. The gold Woolie Bear wears the same outfit in green and beige wool. The smaller Wee Woolie Bear wears only a scarf.

• BEAR ESSENTIALS •

HT: 21in (53cm)

FUR: white, wool pile on polyester backing
EYES: brown, safe, plastic, black pupils
EARS: small, narrow, placed wide apart
MUZZLE: blunt, extends from top of head

NOSE: hand-embroidered, triangular, brown
ARMS: unjointed, no defined paws; no claws
FEET: curving; white plush pads; no claws
STUFFING: synthetic

DAKIN

Trademark

❧ "Knebbyworth" ❧

1985 NAOMI LAIGHT

"Knebbyworth" is the work of British teddy bear artist Naomi Laight, who has made old-style collectors' bears in her home since the early 1980s. The bear's present owner bought him during a Save the Children charity show of bears at Knebworth House, Hertfordshire, in England – hence his name.

EARS
"Knebbyworth's" small ears are folded almost completely in half, and the inner part is sewn into the facial seam. This makes them lie back flat and face outward.

EYES
The large flat black plastic buttons resemble the flat metal buttons used in the early British bear (*see p.30*). These, however, have plastic loops sewn into the face with strong cotton.

NOSE AND MOUTH
Black wool vertical stitches respresent his oval nose. A few stitches in the center extend down to the inverted V-shaped mouth.

CLAWS
Both the feet and the paws have four black wool claws sewn onto the mohair plush.

Long thin muzzle

Bear profile *"Knebbyworth" resembles the bears made before World War I. He has a long pointed nose, small laid-back ears, a slight hump on his back, long limbs, and curved paws.*

TRADEMARK
"Knebbyworth" has a woven cream label sewn onto his back, with the words "A Naomi Laight Collectors' Bear" embroidered in silk.

Long, tapering arms, curved at the paws

Brown suede pads

Large narrow feet

Short-pile mohair plush

• BEAR ESSENTIALS •

FUR: dark khaki, short-pile, mohair plush	**NOSE:** hand-embroidered, oval, black
EYES: large, flat, black, plastic buttons	**ARMS:** long; brown suede pads; claws
EARS: small, folded, lie flat at back of head	**FEET:** large; brown suede pads; claws
MUZZLE: long, thin, extends from forehead	**STUFFING:** gray/beige cotton flock

HT: 13in (33cm)

A Naomi Laight COLLECTORS BEAR

Trademark

❧ "Woody Herman" ❧

1985 APPLAUSE (DESIGNED BY ROBERT RAIKES)

Robert Raikes produces unique teddy bears and other animals, with individually carved wooden faces and feet, in his studio in northern California. Applause, the company that markets his work, was once a division of the Knickerbocker Toy Co. which merged with Wallace Berrie and Co., in 1984. Applause markets this bear as Jamie.

EYES
The small, clear plastic eyes are glued into recesses carved into his wooden face. The pupils are suggested with holes drilled into the wood behind his eyes.

Small flat ears sewn into a seam running around the head

FUR AND STUFFING
The knitted synthetic plush covering "Woody Herman" is a mixture of light brown and black fibers, giving him a tabbylike appearance. He is stuffed with a soft synthetic wadding.

Short, tapered arms, notable for their lack of paw pads and claws

FEET
The feet are not very well defined. The oval, rounded pads are made of smooth wood, lacquered to a golden sheen.

Bear profile *"Woody Herman's" large, rounded head and protruding carved wooden muzzle are offset by a touch of realism – a stubby tail, an unusual feature on a teddy bear.*

Carefully chiseled mouth gives the bear a winsome expression

MUZZLE
The muzzle and nose are all part of a chiseled wooden mask, stained golden brown. The shiny, buttonlike nose is carved out of the same piece of wood and stained black.

ACCESSORIES
A small booklet giving washing instructions, safety standards, and background information on designer Robert Raikes, is sold with this bear.

• BEAR ESSENTIALS •

HT: 9in (23cm)

FUR: brown and black mix, synthetic plush
EYES: small, clear, plastic, glued to wood mask
EARS: small, flat, placed wide apart
MUZZLE: carved wood, stained brown

NOSE: carved wood, round, stained black
ARMS: short, tapered; no pads or claws
FEET: small; brown wooden pads; no claws
STUFFING: synthetic

Trademark

❧ 109 ❧

❧ Brian's Bear ❧

c. 1987 ASQUITHS

Brian's Bear was designed by teddy bear artist and repairer Brian Beacock for Joan Bland of Asquiths, the first store in Britain selling teddy bears exclusively. Asquiths opened in Windsor in 1984, and two more shops followed in Henley-on-Thames and Eton. Brian's Bear is a caricature of the traditional teddy bear.

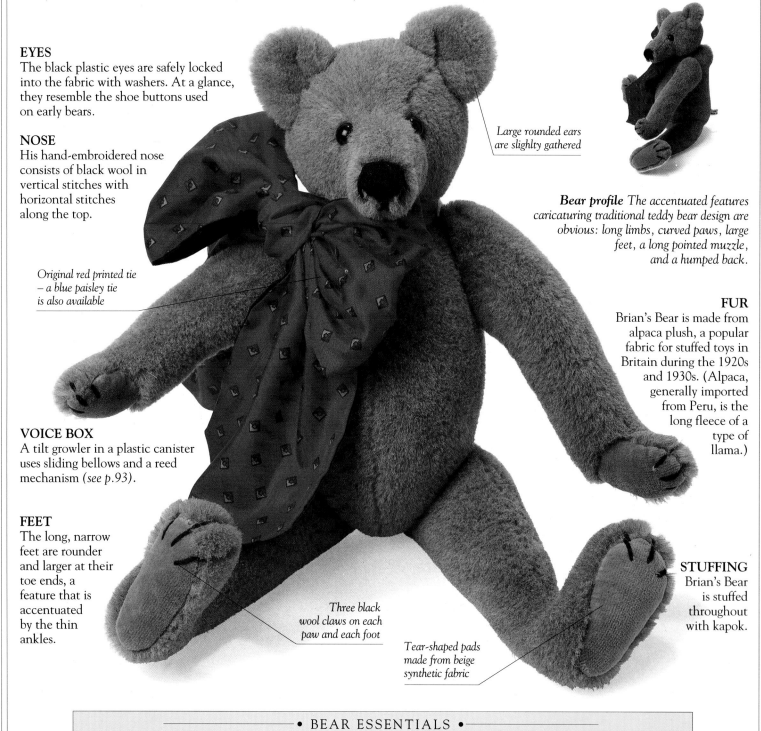

EYES
The black plastic eyes are safely locked into the fabric with washers. At a glance, they resemble the shoe buttons used on early bears.

NOSE
His hand-embroidered nose consists of black wool in vertical stitches with horizontal stitches along the top.

Original red printed tie – a blue paisley tie is also available

VOICE BOX
A tilt growler in a plastic canister uses sliding bellows and a reed mechanism (*see p.93*).

FEET
The long, narrow feet are rounder and larger at their toe ends, a feature that is accentuated by the thin ankles.

Large rounded ears are slighlty gathered

Bear profile *The accentuated features caricaturing traditional teddy bear design are obvious: long limbs, curved paws, large feet, a long pointed muzzle, and a humped back.*

FUR
Brian's Bear is made from alpaca plush, a popular fabric for stuffed toys in Britain during the 1920s and 1930s. (Alpaca, generally imported from Peru, is the long fleece of a type of llama.)

Three black wool claws on each paw and each foot

Tear-shaped pads made from beige synthetic fabric

STUFFING
Brian's Bear is stuffed throughout with kapok.

• BEAR ESSENTIALS •

HT: 16in (40cm)

FUR: fawn-colored, natural alpaca plush
EYES: small, black, safe, plastic, lock-in
EARS: large, rounded, placed high on head
MUZZLE: long, thin, pointed, tapering

NOSE: hand-embroidered, rectangular, black
ARMS: long; beige synthetic pads; claws
FEET: long; beige synthetic pads; claws
STUFFING: synthetic

DISTINGUISHING FEATURES: The smooth alpaca fur is an unusual feature on this bear. His caricatured design and the printed tie are very distinctive.

❧ *Sir Mortimer* ☙

1990 NONSUCH SOFT TOYS

Named after the eminent British archaeologist Sir Mortimer Wheeler, this limited edition bear was created by Susan Rixon to celebrate the 100th anniversary of the excavation of Silchester, a Roman town close to her home in Berkshire, England. Susan and her husband David have been making traditional bears since 1979.

EARS
Sir Mortimer's large and rounded ears are set centrally across the facial seams.

Eyes set wide apart

EYES
Like all of Rixon's teddy bears, Sir Mortimer is equipped with safe, lock-in eyes. They are made of brown plastic.

VOICE BOX
Sir Mortimer contains a tilt growler even though he is not specifically intended for children. Many collectors' bears are made with voice boxes.

Long spoon-shaped pads of orange velvetlike material

FEET
His feet are large and narrow in the traditional style, with long, oval pads of an unusual synthetic, velvet fabric in orange.

Bear profile The elongated muzzle, curved arms, and large feet are based on the traditional teddy bear style, but his slightly arched back reveals no hump.

Long pointed muzzle

NOSE AND MOUTH
Black thread is used for Sir Mortimer's densely stitched nose and mouth.

Original printed bow tie

ARMS
His arms are long, curved, and tapered in the traditional manner. He has especially wide and high-set shoulders.

TRADEMARK
A folded label is set into the back seam. All limited editions have authenticity certificates.

Dark brown, beige, and black mohair plush

• BEAR ESSENTIALS •

FUR: dark brown/beige/black mohair plush
EYES: brown, safe, plastic, black pupils
EARS: large, rounded, over face seams
MUZZLE: very long and pointed
HT: 18in (46cm)

NOSE: hand-embroidered, round, black
ARMS: long; orange synthetic pads; no claws
FEET: large; orange synthetic pads; no claws
STUFFING: synthetic wadding

Nonsuch
Mortimer
Bear ©
Limited Edition
of 200 only

Trademark

❧ *Freddie* ❧

1989 SUE E. FOSKEY

Freddie is one of 400 bears in a limited edition series made by Sue E. Foskey, a teddy bear artist working from home in Delaware, New Jersey. Sue has been designing delightful teddies since 1984; her most recent work includes "antique look" bears, made with distressed mohair and dressed in period clothing.

EARS
Large flat ears sit on the sides of his head. They resemble the ears of Steiff bears made at the beginning of the century.

Thin, pointed muzzle

EYES
Freddie was made for the collectors' market, so he did not have to meet the safety standards required for children's toys. As a result, he has glass bead eyes on wire stalks, similar to those used on small bears in the early years of teddy bear production.

TRADEMARK
Sue Foskey's signature, together with the number of the edition (46/400, showing that he was the 46th bear out of 400 produced) is written on the bear's right foot. His left foot carries a printed label bearing the designer's name and the date of manufacture.

Claws stitched across the plush

FEET
Freddie has large feet with long, narrow, oval pads of beige felt. The four claws are shown with black thread.

Designer's signature and limited edition number

***Bear profile** Freddie's pointed muzzle, thin body, long and tapering arms and legs, and large feet are all features borrowed from earlier bears.*

Black thread mouth

NOSE
His rectangular nose is made up of horizontal stitches of black thread. They are sewn across the tip of his muzzle.

A sharp lilac bow and a tiny cluster of flowers add to Freddie's charms

ARMS
The long tapering arms are relatively wide at the shoulders. The paws are both narrow and curved.

FUR
Freddie is made from brown mohair plush. However, the muzzle is clipped and reveals the woven backing.

• BEAR ESSENTIALS •

HT: 10in (25cm)

FUR: light brown, mohair plush	NOSE: hand-embroidered, rectangular, black
EYES: small, black, glass beads	ARMS: long; beige felt pads; claws
EARS: large, flat, set on sides of head	FEET: large; beige felt pads; claws
MUZZLE: thin, pointed, clipped	STUFFING: kapok throughout bear

Trademark

❦ The Bride ❦

1990 DEE HOCKENBERRY

The Bride was made for the collectors' market. She is a sugar-sweet creation of well-established teddy bear artist Dee Hockenberry, who is based in Albion, New York. A dealer in collectible Steiff animals and teddy bears, Dee is also a well-known writer of books and articles on the subject.

EARS
The Bride's large, flat ears are set wide apart, leaving plenty of room for her elaborate lace and bead headdress.

Protruding muzzle

EYES
Unlike the majority of teddy bears made during this period, The Bride has glass eyes held on wire shanks, reverting to the old style. To comply with safety standards, she carries a warning that reads, "Not for Children under Four."

ACCESSORIES
The Bride's outfit consists of a short, lacy bolero and a headdress of the same material. Both are adorned with artificial flowers and sprays of white plastic pearl-like beads.

Four claws extend across the plush and felt pads

White felt pads match the color of the mohair plush

Bear profile The Bride has a pert, upturned muzzle and large feet reminiscent of the early Steiff bears. Her arms, which bend at the elbow, are a break from tradition.

Amber glass eyes with black pupils

NOSE AND MOUTH
The triangular nose and the mouth are hand-stitched with pinkish-brown embroidery thread. The nose is similar both in style and color to the 1921 white Steiff bear (*see p.42*).

ARMS
The Bride has unusual arms that bend at the elbows. They are a little like Steiff's Teddy Baby of 1930 (*see p.49*).

Folded, printed label, sewn into left leg seam

• BEAR ESSENTIALS •

HT: 13in (33cm)

FUR: white, mohair plush
EYES: medium, amber, glass, black pupils
EARS: large, flat, positioned wide apart
MUZZLE: pert, protruding, and upturned

NOSE: hand-stitched, triangular, pink-brown
ARMS: long, bent; white felt pads; claws
FEET: large, narrow; white felt pads; claws
STUFFING: kapok throughout bear

TRADEMARK: The Bride had a folded, printed label, carrying the artist's name. It was stitched into the seam at the back of her left leg.

THE MODERN BEAR

In recent years teddy bear collecting, or arctophily, has become an internationally recognized hobby. The growing interest in teddy bears has caused auction prices to escalate; in 1989, a Steiff bear was auctioned at Sotheby's for an extraordinary $86,000. Increased demand has led to several cases of fraud, with Steiff or Bing buttons being attached to bears in an attempt to increase value. Today, experts study the history of the teddy bear; collectors' magazines are published in the United States, Great Britain, and Australia, and teddy bear conventions are held, especially in the United States, where events are staged annually in Baltimore, Orlando, San Diego, and Toledo.

A Serious Business

Teddy bears have become serious business, and several museums dedicated to them now exist. Among the best known are Florentine Wagner's collection in Berlin; Colin Wilson's in Queensland, Australia; and in England, Gyles Brandreth's in Stratford-upon-Avon. One of the most recent additions is Franny's Teddy Bear Museum in Florida, which opened in 1990. Several of the major stuffed toy manufacturers now display some of their early samples and they have also published their histories. Steiff has a museum located within its factory complex in Giengen. Merrythought, too, has documented its history, and several of its factory samples are featured at its small museum in the town of Ironbridge, Shropshire, England.

Teddy Bear Restoration

The number of expert restorers has risen in response to the growing demand for repairs to tattered teds saved from the backs of closets and garages. As early as 1972, an amusing survey was written by veterinarians Blackmore and Young entitled "Some Observations of the Diseases of *Brunus Edwardii*." This highly scientific paper discussed, among other problems, cases of soggy ear, ruptured frontal seam, and "alopecia" (hair loss). To deal with these afflictions, special products have been developed for bear care. Teddy bear dust covers and a cleaning fluid made by the Beverly Hills-based Bear Care Co. are two examples.

Traditional Bears

Large manufacturers, such as Steiff, Hermann, Gund, Merrythought, and Dean's, are responding to the passion for old teds by producing traditional hump-backed, long-limbed and muzzled designs, often in limited editions. Other

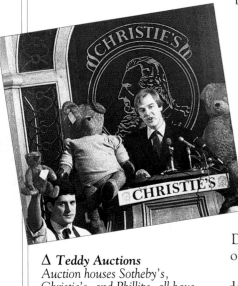

△ **Museum Piece**
A curator at the Bethnal Green Museum of Childhood in London catalogs a new acquisition before putting it on display.

△ **Teddy Auctions**
Auction houses Sotheby's, Christie's, and Phillips, all have sales devoted to teddy bears and other toys. They will make appraisals, unlike the museums.

△ **1930s Replica**
Made by Canterbury Bears, Theodore is a modern bear based on a 1930s design.

▷ **Collectors' Paradise**
Judy Sparrow has an extensive collection on display at her teddy bear museum in Petersfield, Hampshire, England. She also sells modern collectors' bears and runs a repair service for old teddies.

examples of attempts to capture past moments in the teddy bear's history include the delightful Steiff Berryman Bear, based on the cartoonist Berryman's original *Washington Post* illustration and designed by Linda Mullins. The House of Nisbet revived the Schuco-invented Yes/No bears in 1988, and Bedford Bears recently introduced a line of blue bears similar to those popular between the 1930s and 1950s. Steiff pioneered the concept of reproducing bears from its archives for the collectors' market. Replicas are also being made of bears with interesting backgrounds, such as the Steiff "Alfonzo" (*see p.118*) and "Happy" (*see p.45*), "Delicatessen" (*see p.119*), and "Gatti," the little 1907 Bing bear who survived the sinking of the Titanic in 1912.

ANNIVERSARY BEARS

Many older companies are also producing limited edition bears to mark special anniversaries. In 1978 Ideal made a birthday bear to celebrate its 75th anniversary; Hermann did the same to mark its 75th birthday in 1982; Gund celebrated its 85th birthday in 1983, and Merrythought announced 60 years of age in 1990 (*see p.120*). The more recent companies have followed suit: British firms Canterbury Bears (*see p.121*) and Bedford Bears made special bears on their anniversaries in 1990. Some museums have commissioned companies to manufacture bears for them.

△ Toy Store Bear
The Hamley's Bear was specially made by Steiff for Hamley's toy store in London.

REPLICA BEARS

The teddy bear collecting boom of the 1980s, and the accompanying price rise of antique teddy bears at auction, inspired some of the manufacturers to produce replicas of their earlier lines. Their intention was to provide collectors with old-looking bears at more reasonable prices. Ironically many of these replicas are now increasing in value and some are extremely expensive. Steiff, Hermann, and Dean have all produced replicas.

1905 RICHARD STEIFF TEDDY REPLICA
First reproduced in 1980, this little gray bear represents the prototype teddy bear that Richard Steiff developed in 1905. His blunt nose and wide ears were distinguishing features of all bears made at this factory until 1951. Richard Steiff's original bear was placed in the Steiff archives in the 1940s by his mother-in-law. He was one of two gray bears, perhaps made as samples. He is particularly special because his foot was signed in 1983 by Hans Otto Steiff, the great-great-nephew of Margarete Steiff, the inspiration behind the Steiff company.

1909 TEDDY BEAR REPLICA
Replicas of the 1909 teddy bear were first made, in two sizes, in 1984. They were so popular that three more sizes were added. Like the original model, the replica is made of woven mohair plush. His stuffing is not excelsior, but synthetic fibers. To conform with modern safety standards, his eyes, which in 1909 would have been sewn-in shoe buttons, are made of molded plastic, secured into the fabric with a washer. In one ear, there is a yellow and red woven tag with a button sewn in.

Steiff's trademark

Molded plastic eyes

Otto Steiff's signature

1983

1925 TEDDY ROSE REPLICA

This shaggy, pink, mohair plush teddy, first reproduced in 1988, is a replica of Teddy Rose, one of an unusual line of 5,000 bears made by Steiff from 1925-1930. Unlike the previous two replicas described, Teddy Rose was made as a limited edition of 10,000 worldwide, a point noted on the bear's printed cardboard chest label. The number (0170) refers to the product. This is followed by the bear's height in centimeters (41). The reverse of the label carries the number of this particular edition; this is reproduced on the guarantee of authenticity certificate that accompanies the bear in a special presentation box. A smaller Teddy Rose, 10 inches in height, was made in a limited edition of 8,000 in 1990. Like the larger replica, he has compact, excelsior stuffing that makes him heavy.

STEIFF
Teddy Rose
Replica 1925
Ltd. Ed. 10 000
1987–1988

△ Cardboard Chest Labels
A modernized cardboard chest label is similar to those used on 1928-1950 bears.

1908 STEIFF SNAP-APART-BEAR REPLICA

First reproduced in 1990, this unusual bear is a replica of an original factory sample for the 1908 Druckknopf (snap fastener) Bär 5353, who was never sold to the public. Snap fasteners had been invented by Carl August Pfenning of Germany in 1895. Their intended use was to button the flies on men's trousers! Steiff borrowed the new invention to produce a series of seven soft toys for young children. These toys consist of a round body with head and limbs attached by snaps. When the head and limbs are removed, the toy becomes a rather unusual ball for throwing. This little white bear is only 7 inches high when complete. When he is pulled apart, you can see Carl Pfenning's patent number clearly impressed around each snap. Along with a golliwog, this bear was one of Steiff's very first experiments. In 1909, this ingenious design was patented as one of Steiff's Roly Poly Toys.

Steiff's button-in-ear trademark

Snap-off arms

1908 "ALFONZO": FRIEND OF A RUSSIAN PRINCESS

In 1908, George Mikhailovich, the Grand Duke of Russia, commissioned Steiff to make this bear for his daughter, Princess Xenia Georgievna. His owner took him to England in 1914, where they were guests of the Russian princess's royal relatives at Buckingham Palace. The outbreak of World War I prevented the princess and her bear from returning home, an event that saved Princess Xenia from certain death in the Russian Revolution. "Alfonzo" became a treasured possession as he was the only gift that she had brought from her homeland, given to her by the father she adored. "Alfonzo's" rarity, and his unusual background, accounted for the fact that he was sold at a Christie's auction in May 1989 for $19,800, then a world record. From the London auction house, he traveled to his new home in the Cotswold village of Witney, near Oxford, England, where he is presently on permanent display at his owner's antique and collectors' teddy bear shop. "Alfonzo" is a unique Steiff bear made of a short rust-red mohair plush, with beige felt paws. His nose is slightly worn and the holes in his paws reveal his traditional excelsior stuffing.

1990 "ALFONZO": REPLICA

Following the purchase of the unique "Alfonzo," the new owners made an arrangement with the present Steiff company to produce a replica bear that they could sell exclusively in their shop, where a number of other collector bears were already available. The replica "Alfonzo" was first produced in a limited edition of 5,000 in 1990. See how faithfully he follows the original: he is the same height, 13 inches and he wears an identical white-trimmed, orange cotton sateen suit, with trousers held up by suspenders, beneath a contemporary Russian-style tunic with a side fastening. Although he is not as worn as the real "Alfonzo," his unusual red plush has a similar light brown woven backing. The "Alfonzo" replica is packed in a stylish dark green presentation box, with his history and the edition number printed on a special certificate of authenticity. The large brass-colored metal button, with incised cursive script, and the white printed collectors' tag in the ear indicate that he is a replica. The original "Alfonzo" has the smaller nickel 1905-1950 button with raised capital letters.

Rust-red mohair plush

Russian-style tunic

Steiff's button-in-ear trademark

Worn felt pad

1907 "ALOYSIUS": BRIDESHEAD HERO

Like "Alphonzo," "Delicatessen" is a much-traveled bear. He began life in about 1907, possibly in the New York-based, Ideal Toy Co. factory. In 1969, he was given to the late British actor and arctophile Peter Bull, following his television appearance on the American *Tonight Show*. Peter Bull christened him "Delicatessen." A little over a decade later, however, the bear's name was officially changed by popular demand, to "Aloysius," following his acting debut as Sebastian's teddy bear in the British television series based on Evelyn Waugh's *Brideshead Revisited*. Filming took him to Venice and the United States. When Peter Bull died in 1984, "Aloysius" was bequeathed to the actor's friend Don Busby and later displayed in the Teddy Bear Museum in Stratford-upon-Avon, England. This world-famous octogenarian returned to his homeland in 1989 to reside with his present owners, American teddy collectors Rosemary and Paul Volpp.

▽ *Brideshead Star*
"Aloysius" in the television series Brideshead Revisited.

1987 "ALOYSIUS": REPLICA

Many of "Delicatessen's" features had already been copied by the House of Nisbet in its Bully Bear *(see p.102)*, but it was not until his television success that a replica was made in 1987. The distressed mohair plush, seen on the replica below, is used by several contemporary makers of traditional teddy bears. It was invented by Nisbet's Jack Wilson, in conjunction with Norton (Weaving) Ltd. of Yorkshire, using a 1904 velvet-crushing machine. The chamois leather patches on the limbs and body of the replica bear are identical to those on the original; indeed the likeness, in general, is so close that it is really only the House of Nisbet woven label that gives away the replica bear's identity. Each replica comes with a copy of the scarf presented to the bear by the wife of his costar, Anthony Andrews, and a British Airways flight bag, denoting his well-traveled career. Originally the replicas were to be called "Aloysius" but the North American Bear Co. had already bought the copyright for reproducing the bear, and so the replica used the bear's original name, "Delicatessen."

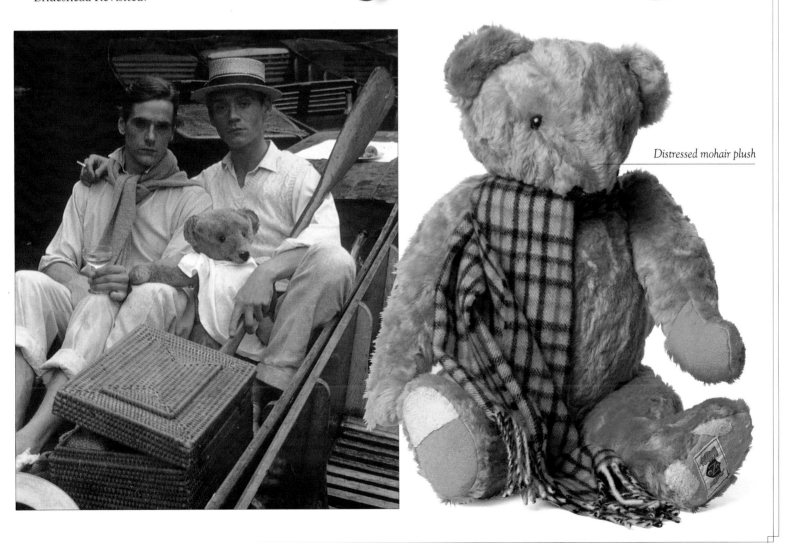

Distressed mohair plush

ANNIVERSARY BEARS

This special limited edition bear was produced to mark the 60th birthday of Merrythought Ltd., one of the oldest surviving British stuffed toy manufacturers. Similar in style to 1930s designs, the Diamond Jubilee Bear was introduced in June 1990 at Harrods. He comes in a royal blue presentation box. He has a limited edition tag signed by the company's managing director, grandson of the firm's founder, stitched into his left seam.

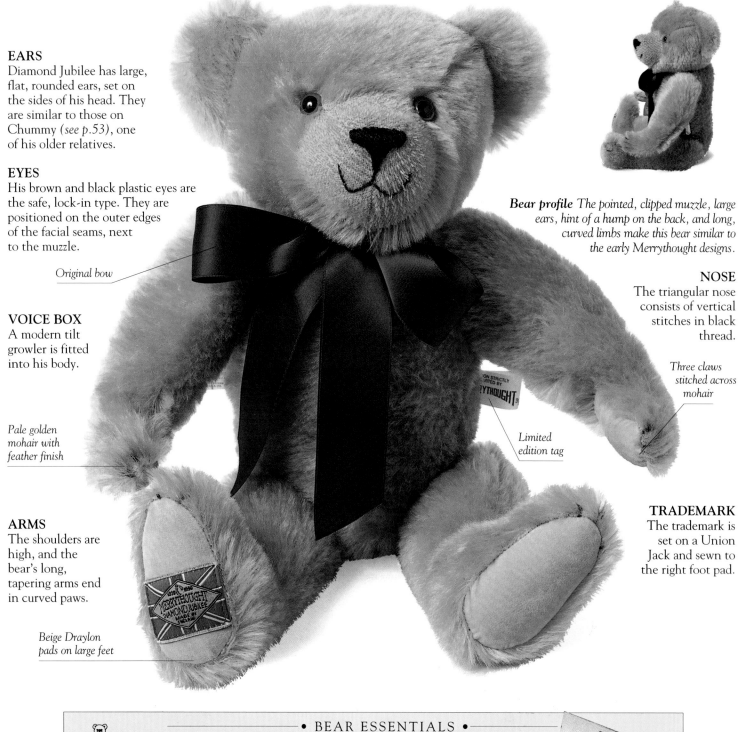

EARS
Diamond Jubilee has large, flat, rounded ears, set on the sides of his head. They are similar to those on Chummy (*see p.53*), one of his older relatives.

EYES
His brown and black plastic eyes are the safe, lock-in type. They are positioned on the outer edges of the facial seams, next to the muzzle.

Original bow

VOICE BOX
A modern tilt growler is fitted into his body.

Pale golden mohair with feather finish

ARMS
The shoulders are high, and the bear's long, tapering arms end in curved paws.

Beige Draylon pads on large feet

Bear profile The pointed, clipped muzzle, large ears, hint of a hump on the back, and long, curved limbs make this bear similar to the early Merrythought designs.

NOSE
The triangular nose consists of vertical stitches in black thread.

Three claws stitched across mohair

Limited edition tag

TRADEMARK
The trademark is set on a Union Jack and sewn to the right foot pad.

• BEAR ESSENTIALS •

HT: 18in (48cm)

FUR: pale gold, mohair plush, some clipped
EYES: amber, safe, plastic, black pupils
EARS: large, flat, rounded, on sides of head
MUZZLE: protruding, pointed, clipped

NOSE: hand-embroidered, triangular, black
ARMS: long, tapering; beige Draylon pads; claws
FEET: large; beige Draylon pads; claws
STUFFING: excelsior; polyester

Trademark

PRIVATE ISSUE NOT FOR RESALE

Launched in April 1990, this large bear celebrates the 10th anniversary of a family business, based just outside the ancient cathedral city of Canterbury, in Kent, England. The firm produces 50,000 bears a year, but the anniversary bear is one of a limited edition of just 500. The 10th Anniversary Bear follows the traditional teddy bear design; he has long limbs, a humped back, and a pointed nose.

Close-set eyes

EARS
The small, rounded ears are placed in the corners of his large, squarish head. The inside of the ear is made from the same suede fabric that is used for the foot and paw pads.

EYES
His amber and black, plastic, lock-in eyes are set low down on his face, giving him a high forehead.

Original bow

FEET
The feet are large. Maude and John Blackburn, who own Canterbury Bears, have signed the suede pad on his right foot.

CLAWS
Each black wool claw is indicated with two stitches: one stitch reaches across the suede pad; the other stretches across the mohair plush.

Three black wool claws on each paw

Large suede pads

Thin, black wool mouth

Bear profile *Like so many modern collector's bears, he is a caricature of traditional teddy design, with his humped back, long limbs, and protruding, pointed muzzle.*

NOSE
The nose is hand-embroidered. Vertical stitches of black wool create a slightly wider nose than those found on other bears manufactured by this firm.

ARMS
His arms are exceptionally long, and they are placed very high on his body. They taper and curve into long, beige, suede-padded paws.

TRADEMARK
A woven label featuring Canterbury City's Coat of Arms, an honour bestowed on the firm in 1987, is sewn into the left side seam.

Five claws on each foot

• BEAR ESSENTIALS •

HT: 66cm (26in)

FUR: biscuit coloured, mohair plush
EYES: small, amber, safe, plastic, black pupils
EARS: small, rounded, suede inner ear
MUZZLE: protruding, pointed

NOSE: hand-embroidered, rectangular, black
ARMS: long, tapering, large suede pads; claws
FEET: large; oval suede pads; claws
STUFFING: polyester

Trademark

THE WORKING BEAR

Teddy Roosevelt's bear began life as a mascot, and the tradition continues today, with teddy bears lending their support to political, sports, and charitable causes. Rupert Bear, for example, is used to promote a charity that helps people suffering from muscular dystrophy, and Paddington Bear has a club that contributes to the British charity Action Research for the Crippled Child. There is no doubt that, over the years, the teddy bear has assumed an important role as a universal comforter and a symbol of friendship and security.

GOOD BEARS OF THE WORLD

Many unique teddy bears have been produced in recent times to help children with special needs. There are bears designed to help fretful babies sleep: The Kamar Toy Co.'s Dear Heart Bear has a battery-operated heart that beats like a human mother's. There is also a bear made to help the profoundly deaf; his red eyes light up when he "hears." In England, Bill Bear was designed for chemical-sensitive children by Mary Holden, a fellow sufferer. Teddy bears have also proved a powerful support in distressing situations. In one French hospital, for example, prior to surgery, children are guided through an operation using their teddy bears as patients, to help dispel fear. In the United States, the police in Colorado use the Celestial Seasonings Tea Co.'s Sleepy Time Bear to help young victims of accident and abuse.

The teddy bear's role as soulmate and confessor led to the founding of Good Bears of the World, an international fund-raising organization providing

△ **Olympic Mascot**
The 1980 Olympic Games used Mishka, a bear from Russian folklore, as a mascot.

△ **Bear for the Disabled**
Made in the United States, these bears are designed to help disabled children come to terms with their handicaps.

◁ **Tom Foolery**
A limited edition of 150 Tom Foolery bears were made for Disney World's Second Annual Teddy Bear Convention in Florida, in 1989. The bears were made by Doris and Terry Michaud.

teddy bears for hospitalized children and adults, as well as the old and frail in nursing homes, and children in foster homes. The brainchild of American journalist James T. Ownby, it was inaugurated in Bern, Switzerland, in 1973. Until Ownby's death in 1986, the organization was based at his home in Honolulu, Hawaii, but it now operates from Ohio. There are over 10,000 worldwide members, organized into groups – "dens" – that buy and distribute teddy bears to worthy causes.

FUND-RAISING

In the United States, the official Good Bears of the World Bear was made by Ideal in the 1980s, and now by Dakin. Theodore Roosevelt's birthday, October 27, has been designated Good Bear Day, and so fund-raising events involving teddies often occur then. In Britain, however, the first great teddy bear rally was on May 27, 1979, when 15,000 people and 2,000 teddy bears met on the grounds of Longleat, the Wiltshire home of the Marquis of Bath and his teddy bear, "Clarence." It initiated more rallies in England, as well as in New Zealand and Australia. In the United States, teddy bear conventions, where enthusiasts meet to exchange ideas, stories, and bears, are particularly popular. Teddy bears are also used for fund-raising. In Britain, for example, the sale of a white bear called "William" raises money for the Royal Marsden, a prominent cancer hospital, and Merrythought's replica of a teddy bear owned by British actress Dame Judi Dench raises money for the Child Psychotherapy Trust.

△ Police Help
Teddy bears, often donated by Good Bears of the World, are used by police officers to help traumatized children talk about their experiences.

△ Charity Work
Pudsey Bear is the official symbol for BBC television's annual Children in Need charity appeal.

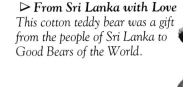

▷ From Sri Lanka with Love
This cotton teddy bear was a gift from the people of Sri Lanka to Good Bears of the World.

△ The Marquis of Bath
Residents of Longleat.

△ Teddy Bears Picnic
Bears belonging to the late Colonel Bob Henderson, founder of the UK branch of Good Bears of the World, and a leading light in arctophily.

CARE AND REPAIR

A teddy bear suffers from too much loving – he may lose an eye or an ear, his joints may weaken from being constantly held by one limb, or his stuffing might sag from being slept on for so many years. Minor operations may be performed at home, although it is always best to seek advice. Bears can be lightly sponged with a diluted mild detergent, or brushed to remove surface dust, but they should never be completely submerged. Fortunately the number of expert restorers has increased over the last few years to meet the growing demand of time-ravaged teds. Detached limbs, unthreading noses, and mute growlers can all be resurrected, with care and patience.

EVERYDAY BEAR CARE

It is worth remembering that a teddy is a textile, and he is therefore affected by light, dust, moisture, and the combined traumas of everyday life – insects, vermin, bacteria, and most common of all, overly affectionate children and dogs. Although the fibers of the materials will weaken and discolor with time, the following tips should prevent any further major damage. Keep your bear away from direct sunlight; make him clothes or change his position occasionally; gently vacuum or dust him regularly. Store him in a dry atmosphere, at a constant temperature, since warm, damp conditions encourage mold. Check him for insect life, such as the larvae of the carpet beetle, which leave a cobweblike trail and oval casings. If any are found, seal the teddy in a plastic bag with mothballs.

EYES

Lock-in eyes make the best replacements for a child's toy. Historical accuracy, however, dictates the more appropriate glass eyes. The wire shank is sewn in position, and a long needle takes the strong thread through to the back of the head to be fastened off.

NOSE AND MOUTH

Thick embroidery silk is ideal for nose repair, although wool can be used if care is taken to match the new thread to any original stitches.

GROWLER

Tilt growlers are removed through the bear's back seam. A new one may require padding out with extra stuffing.

EARS

Ears are frequently torn or lost. This bear has a new ear, made from a similar plush. It is oversewn into place, ensuring that its position matches the other ear.

PAINTED PADS

English bears made between about 1930 and the late 1950s often had pads of Rexine, an oilcloth that is no longer available. A similar fabric can be created by painting a muslin-type material with quick-drying brown paint. It can be cut to size and sewn in place.

ALL SEWN UP

If a bear loses an arm or leg, a new one can be made from a similar piece of plush, matching the design to the remaining limb. Here a section of plush is machine-stitched on the wrong side, leaving a gap at the shoulder end so that the stuffing and joints can be inserted.

PATCHING UP

The plush often wears thin at points where the bear has been constantly cuddled, or moth holes may develop over a period of time. Patching is best done beneath the hole rather than over the top, either by neatly oversewing into place or using invisible stitching.

JOINTS

A cardboard disk and washer with a cotter pin inserted through the center has been replaced. The pin will be pushed through the lower part of the body and then through the corresponding washer and disk behind it.

STUFFING

Teddies often have the stuffing quite literally knocked out of them. Excelsior is ground to powder, or the kapok loses its youthful plumpness. The new stuffing can be inserted through one of the final handsewn seams.

FELT PADS

Felt pads can suffer from moths – or simply come apart at the seams. The felt has been removed from this bear, and the new matching felt has been cut to size and neatly oversewn into place.

INDEX

PAINTED PADS
English bears made between about 1930 and the late 1950s often had pads of Rexine, an oilcloth that is no longer available. A similar fabric can be created by painting a muslin-type material with quick-drying brown paint. It can be cut to size and sewn in place.

ALL SEWN UP
If a bear loses an arm or leg, a new one can be made from a similar piece of plush, matching the design to the remaining limb. Here a section of plush is machine-stitched on the wrong side, leaving a gap at the shoulder end so that the stuffing and joints can be inserted.

PATCHING UP
The plush often wears thin at points where the bear has been constantly cuddled, or moth holes may develop over a period of time. Patching is best done beneath the hole rather than over the top, either by neatly oversewing into place or using invisible stitching.

JOINTS
A cardboard disk and washer with a cotter pin inserted through the center has been replaced. The pin will be pushed through the lower part of the body and then through the corresponding washer and disk behind it.

STUFFING
Teddies often have the stuffing quite literally knocked out of them. Excelsior is ground to powder, or the kapok loses its youthful plumpness. The new stuffing can be inserted through one of the final handsewn seams.

FELT PADS
Felt pads can suffer from moths – or simply come apart at the seams. The felt has been removed from this bear, and the new matching felt has been cut to size and neatly oversewn into place.

INDEX

Acknowledgments

Dorling Kindersley would like to thank the following, who generously lent their bears and associated memorabilia for special photography:
Timothy Atkinson 74; Brian Beacock 14, 15, 36, 37, 72, 73, 92, 93; Bear Essentials 97; Bethnal Green Museum of Childhood (a branch of the Victoria and Albert Museum) 5, 11, 13, 16, 17, 38, 39, 41, 47, 59, 82, 89, 98, 99, 100, 101, 102, 104, 106; Heather Bischoff 28, 31; Gyles Brandreth, Teddy Bear Museum, Stratford-upon-Avon half-title page, title page, 6, 10, 11, 16, 18, 22, 23, 24, 38, 46, 69, 75, 76, 77, 78, 81, 94, 95, 96, 97, 111, 122, 123; Canterbury Bears 11, 103, 114; Pauline Cockrill 8, 9, 11, 67, 71, 72, 73, 79, 92, 93; Faith Eaton 11, 44; Nancy Evans 8, 11, 88; Lucinda Ganderton 8, 74, 75; Paul Goble 11, 49; Pam Hebbs title page, 5, 8, 9, 10, 11, 13, 16, 17, 18, 19, 21, 32, 34, 35, 38, 40, 42, 63, 71, 75, 77, 96, 97, 112, 113, 116, 117, 122; Peter Hebbs 97; Gillian Lister 66; London Toy and Model Museum 12, 86, 87; Merrythought Ltd. 120; Sheryl Nairn 50, 51; Ian Pout, "Teddy Bears" 5, 10, 11, 19, 33, 39, 40, 41, 64, 70, 118; Private Collection 5, 9, 10, 11, 17, 38, 60, 61, 62, 77, 85, 94, 95, 96, 107, 108, 109, 117, 119; David Robinson 8, 75; John Smith, The Doll's Hospital, Fulham, London 14, 15, 36, 37, 72, 73, 92, 93; Judy Sparrow, The Bear Museum, Petersfield 7, 10, 11, 18, 19, 30, 34, 35, 40, 41, 43, 48, 52, 53, 54, 55, 58, 71, 76, 83, 105, 114, 115, 124, 125; Paul and Rosemary Volpp 5, 11, 13, 20, 25, 26, 27, 29, 45, 65, 68, 69, 80, 119; Lynnet Wilson 8, 11, 84.

Thanks also to the following whose bears are currently on loan to the Teddy Bear Museum, Stratford-upon-Avon: Mike Reid (Sooty glove puppet) 76; Michael Bond (Paddington and bed) 86; Barbara Cartland (the Prince of Love) 90.

We are indebted to Irene Lyford, Damien Moore and Helen Townsend for their invaluable editorial help, and Marcus Hardy and Gillian Prince for additional editorial assistance; to Kate Grant and Susan Thompson for preliminary research; and to Emma Matthews for keying-in the text.

The author would like to thank the following people for all their help and advice:
Jacki Brooks of the Australian Doll Digest; Sylvia Coote; Glenn Jackman; Pat Rush; Pam Howells; John Blackburn of Canterbury Bears; Oliver Holmes of Merrythought Ltd.; Michael Crane of Dean's (1903) Company; Diane Phillips of Collins; Bunny Campione of Sotheby's; Judy and John Sparrow; Pam and Peter Hebbs; Brenda and Frank Faris; staff of the Bethnal Green Museum of Childhood; Sheryl and Mrs. Nairn; John Smith of the Fulham Doll's Hospital; Brian Beacock; Joan Bland of Asquiths; Ian Pout of "Teddy Bears"; Sue Rixon of Nonsuch Soft Toys; Naomi Laight; Rosemary Volpp; Denise Naylor of the X-ray Department of Kingston Hospital, Kingston upon Thames, Surrey; Sister Marie Claire; Michael Morse; Heather Bischoff; Tracie Vallis; Felix C. Sear; Trevor Williamson; Bear & Friends, Brighton.

Special thanks to the curatorial staff of Bethnal Green Museum of Childhood for their support, and also to numerous family and friends, in particular Ruth Cornett, Kevin Edge, and especially Lynnet Wilson and "Cully" who started the ball rolling.

Picture Credits

Archiv/INTERFOTO 10, 12; Associated Press/Christie's 114; Bethnal Green Museum of Childhood 114; Camera Press 122, 123; Frank Spooner 122, 123; The Hulton-Deutsch Collection 12; © MPL 51; National Portrait Gallery, London 56; Popperfoto 35, 57, 71; Ian Pout 19; Rex Features 90; Smithsonian Institute 13; Sotheby's 6; Steiff Museum 12, 34; Topham Picture Library 56, 70, 91, 123; Ullstein Bilderdienst 34; Courtesy of the Trustees of the V&A 5, 10, 11, 13, 16, 17, 38, 39, 41, 59, 82, 89, 98, 99, 100, 101, 102, 104, 106; Paul & Rosemary Volpp 7, 119.

BRIDESHEAD REVISITED picture, Granada Television 119, reproduced with kind permission of Anthony Andrews and Jeremy Irons.

Special photography by Roland Kemp.
Additional photography by Pip Barnard, Jim Coit (in the USA), and Tim Ridley.

Watercolor illustrations by Pauline Baynes; black and white line drawings by Peter Serjeant.

Colored line illustrations by Peggy Fortnum from PADDINGTON'S NOTEBOOK and PADDINGTON STORYBOOK by Michael Bond 86, 87. Reprinted by kind permission of Harper Collins Publishers Limited.

Line illustrations from WINNIE-THE-POOH © E.H. Shepard under the Berne Convention, in the United States © 1926 by E.P. Dutton & Co. Inc., © renewal 1954 by A.A. Milne. Coloring-in © 1970 by E.H. Shepard and Methuen & Co. Ltd., © 1973 by E.H. Shepard and Methuen Children's Books Ltd. 56, 57. Line illustration from THE HOUSE AT POOH CORNER © E.H. Shepard under the Berne Convention, in the United States © 1928 by E.P. Dutton & Co. Inc., © renewal 1956 by A.A. Milne. Coloring-in © 1974 by E.H. Shepard and Methuen Children's Books Ltd. 56. Reproduced by permission of Curtis Brown, London.

Rupert illustrations 50, 51 reproduced by kind permission of Express Newspapers plc.

Useful Addresses

The Bear Museum
38 Dragon Street
Petersfield
Hampshire GU31 4JJ
England
Telephone (0730) 65108/66962

Bethnal Green Museum of Childhood
Cambridge Heath Road
London E2 9PA
England
Telephone (081) 981 1711/6789

Frannie's Teddy Bear Museum
2511 Pine Ridge Road
Naples, Florida 33942
U.S.A.
Telephone (813) 598 2711

Good Bears of the World
2352 Valeway Drive
Toledo, Ohio 43613
U.S.A.

Margaret Woodbury Strong Museum
1 Manhattan Square
Rochester, New York 14607
U.S.A.
Telephone (716) 263 2700

The Steiff Museum
Margarete Steiff GmbH
PO Box 1560
Alliin Strasse 2
D-7928
Giengen (Brenz)
West Germany
Telephone (49) 7322 1311

The Teddy Bear Museum
19 Greenhill Street
Stratford-upon-Avon
Warwickshire CV37 6LF
England
Telephone (0789) 293160

Magazines

Hugglets Teddy Bear Magazine
Glenn Jackman
PO Box 290
Brighton BN2 1DR
England
Telephone (0273) 697974

The Teddy Bear and Friends
Hobby House Press
900 Frederick Street
Cumberland, Maryland 21502
U.S.A.
Telephone (301) 759 3770

Teddy Bear Times
Ashdown Publishing
Shelley House
104 High Street
Steyning
West Sussex BN4 3RD
England
Telephone (0903) 816111